The book of green tea

W9-BXL-820

The book of green tea

Text by Christine Dattner • Photographs by Sophie Boussahba
Designed by Emmanuelle Javelle

UNIVERSE

© Archipel studio, 2002
produced by Archipel studio
10, rue Louis-Bertrand – 94200 Ivry-sur-Seine

Editor : Jean-Jacques Brisebarre
Art director : Thomas Brisebarre
Editorial assistant : Juliette Neveux

First published in the United States of America in 2003
by UNIVERSE PUBLISHING
A Division of Rizzoli International Publications, Inc.
300 Park Avenue South
New York, NY 10010

© 2003 by Universe Publishing

All rights reserved. No part of this publication may be
reproduced, stored in a retrieval system, or transmitted in any form
or by any means, electronic, mechanical, photocopying, recording,
or otherwise, without prior consent of the publishers.

2003 2004 2005 2006 2007 / 10 9 8 7 6 5 4 3 2 1

Printed in E.U.

ISBN: 0-7893-0853-3

Library of Congress Catalog Control Number: 2002112177

Table of Contents

Preface

Come oh come
Ye thirsty restless ones,
The kettle is on
It sings and bubbles
Musically

RABINDRANATH TAGORE

Previous pages: Japanese
cast-iron teapot and teacup;
Enameled stoneware
Chinese teapot and teacup;
Braid of China black tea;
Arita porcelain Japanese set
with Bancha Hojicha roasted
green tea.

Left: Fuji-Yama Japanese
cast-iron teapot and
stoneware teacup.

A gift from nature, tea is a treasure that is comparable to wine in its diversity, its cultivation, its flavors and its manifold origins. Tea is part of the history of mankind, like a rhythm that accompanies human life. The preparation and uses of tea and the approaches to drinking it have varied over time. Legend has it that the beverage was discovered in China by a "Divine Cultivator" who immediately made it the national drink, attributing many curative virtues to the beverage (already!) Tea was the first ingredient to be added to heated water, before becoming a staple in the cuisines of China (until the end of the Tang dynasty), as well as in Korean and Tibetan cooking. Under the Song dynasty, tea was boiled in water. It was first infused during the Ming dynasty as it still is today.

Along with these developments, tea became a philosophy, a way of life, and a basic element in several religions. When Lu Yu wrote his first *Treatise on Tea* during the Tang dynasty, he inspired Taoism. In the sixteenth century, Sen No Rikyu wrote the Cha No Yu (the code of the Japanese tea ceremony) in Kyoto, emphasizing the refinement of tea and the arts that accompanied it (kakemono, *ikebana* and ceramics) and making the rites of tea preparation an integral part of the Zen religion.

Introduced to the West in the seventeenth century, tea cast its spell over Europe. It quickly became an important factor in politics, society and economics, playing a role in the American Revolution and the Opium War in China.

The Crimean War led the English to turn their attention toward new export markets, resulting in the introduction of tea to North Africa and then to the rest of the continent.

7

Such events, marked by conflict, violence and human tragedy, lend a poignant bitterness to tea, as if the infusion were tainted with the color of blood.

After prevailing as a British monopoly for a long time in Europe, tea began to distance itself from London and experienced a renaissance at the end of the twentieth century, finding important new outlets in cosmetics and chilled prepared beverages. Tea has made major inroads in new markets, spurred by highly effective advertising campaigns and publicity. Physicians, increasingly inclined to respect the curative powers of traditional remedies, have incorporated tea into regimes to garner its health benefits.

But tea has not lost its soul. It has discovered and demonstrated its adaptability to the modern world through the emergence of shops, cafés, and salons specializing in tea. These are generally refined, simple and authentic spots, where the rich diversity of tea is emphasized and celebrated.

The tea connoisseur can travel anew along the *Cha Do*, to discover or rediscover this extraordinary beverage: its rituals, demands, and infinite riches, together with its simple pleasures. There are countless tea ceremonies, each different from the next, ranging from Gung *Fu Cha* in the mists of the Hangzhou Lake to the minted green tea of the Moroccan Berbers, the *Cha No Yu* of Kyoto, the tea of the Baïkal caravans in Samarkand, and the tea drawn from samovars in Saint Petersburg or Kabul. Tea ceremonies are living theatre, inviting participation with a gesture of welcome; these rituals are symbols of friendship and hospitality, offering a profound understanding of tea.

Black teas predominated in Europe through most of the twentieth century, but today there is once again a vast selection; green tea has regained popularity and in its wake, the Oolongs (semi-fermented teas), with their surpassingly delicate flavors, have gained admirers. At the same time, flowery, fruity and flavored teas, an ancient tradition in China—think back to the legendary "eight treasure tea"—are enjoyed by more than a third of tea drinkers.

"Humanity has always rediscovered itself over a cup of tea," wrote Okakura Kakuzo. Christine Dattner, the author of *Tales of Tea*, takes us on a journey toward that destination, or perhaps we should say toward the spirit of humanism, imbued with pleasure and art.

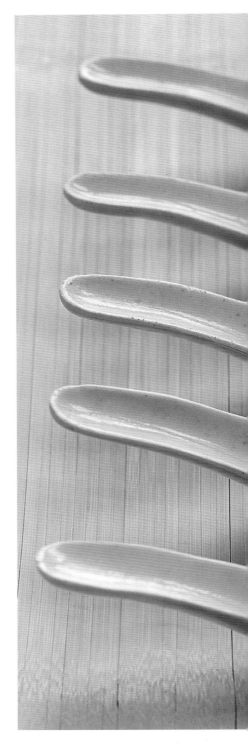

Let her be your guide as she leads you through these pages about tea, which has inspired so much curiosity and passion through the ages. Beyond its comparable flavors and lore, tea is accompanied by the riches of the arts that complement it: flower arranging, calligraphy, and poetry, and the arts of flavors, cuisine, and table arrangement. They lend the drink a timeless, yet ephemeral, quality. Exquisite settings are part of tea's essence; consider the tea boxes and teapots of cast-iron, clay, porcelain, and other ceramic objects.

You will find tea served in the impoverished streets of Calcutta and in the hushed luxury of a Parisian tea salon. It might be prepared in a tea ceremony in Pusan, Shanghai or Kyoto. It may be savored in solitude ("I drink tea to forget the noise of the world," said T'ien Yi Heng) or enjoyed with friends and family ("Nanny, I want some tea!" wrote Anton Chekov). Sometimes the occasion is a delightfully intimate get-together ("They sat around a table, sipping tea and speaking of love," recounted Henrich Heine). Tea is an invitation to a voyage, to reflection, to meditation, to heedfulness of others.

In some countries, it is customary to smilingly offer tea before even speaking words of greeting and welcome. The world is indeed in need of such an offering of green gold, like an olive branch of peace. This aspect of tea is not a utopian, imaginary thing; the way of tea leads us toward a destination of harmony, purity, respect and tranquility. Let us embark without delay on this journey, guided by Christine Dattner, heeding her straightforward advice on how best to prepare it.

"Tea is nothing more than this: heat the water, prepare the tea, and drink it in the proper manner. That is all you need to understand," taught Sen No Rikyu.

As the author explores the special lore of green tea, allow yourself to be lulled as if by soothing murmurs and find yourself adrift "in the flavor of tea, like a subtle spell." In the words of Lu Tung, "Raise your cup to your lips and sip, and you will enter paradise."

Flavored Sencha green teas
in glazed clay spoons.
From top to bottom: Pastoral
Symphony, Syracuse, Green
Paradise, Samurai, Cupidon.

OLIVIER SCALA
Expert tea taster
and President of the Comité français du thé

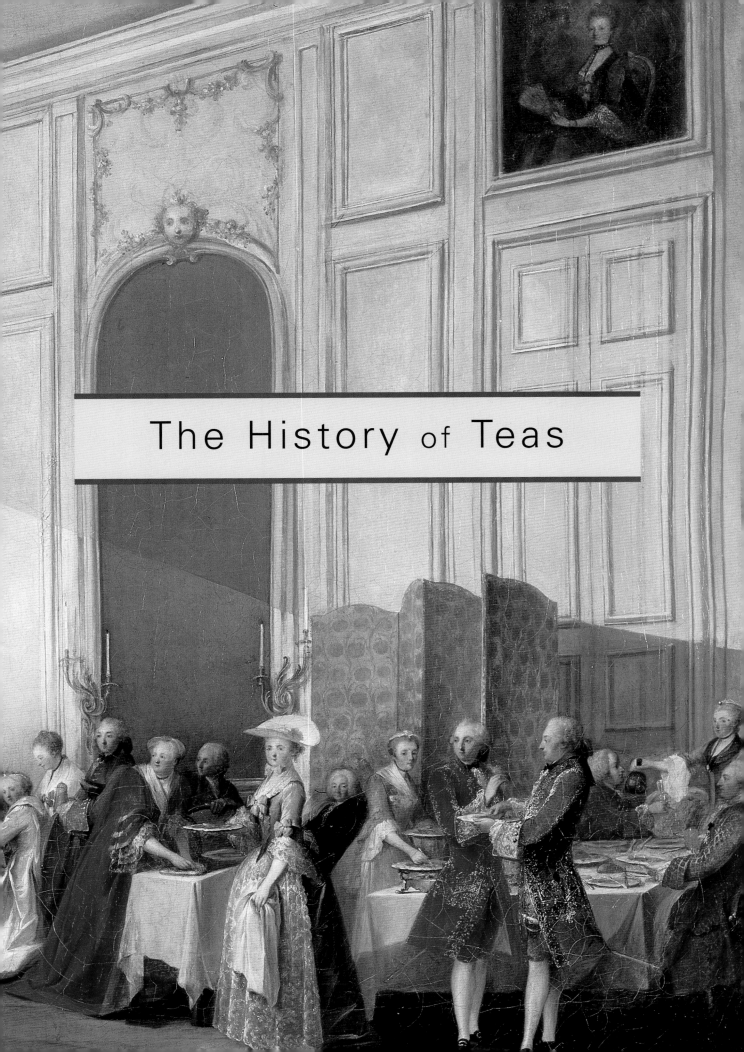

The History of Teas

The birth of tea civilization

Tea was born from the play of wind with nature. Its history begins in China in 2737 B.C. during the reign of the emperor Chen Nung. The monarch was a careful man, attentive to his health, and always boiled water before drinking it. Legend tells how he fell asleep in the shade of a small tree one day, wearied by a long walk. As he dozed, a soft breeze blew down several leaves, which drifted into his pot. When he awoke, the emperor tasted the tinted water and found it delicious. In the centuries since then, the preparation of tea has truly evolved into a way of life.

From China to Japan

Scattered records make it clear that tea was consumed in certain regions of China as early as the first century A.D. However, it was really during the Tang dynasty (618–907 A.D.) that tea consumption became widespread. At that time, tea leaves were compacted into bricks, which were softened by heat before being grated into a powder that was added to the boiling water.

Compressing the leaves helped preserve them and made them easier to transport. These bricks also served as currency in trade with distant lands. Even today in many tea shops, customers can purchase bricks of China black tea weighing about 2.6 lbs. They are so decorative that few have the heart to break them up, choosing instead to preserve them with a protective light coat of varnish.

During this period of Chinese history, Lu Yu (733–804), a Buddhist monk, composed the first *Treatise on Tea*, which earned him the honorific title "the God of Tea." He described the preparation of tea and the delights of drinking it, and recorded details about tea plantations and methods of tea cultivation and processing. Tea had become a noble art on the same level as calligraphy, poetry and painting.

Describing himself as "mad for tea," the poet Lu Tung dedicated himself to the beverage with genuine passion. Among many other homages, he composed a magnificent *Song of Tea*:

To honor tea, I blocked my gate with leafy boughs,
Lest the noisy crowd disturb me,
And I took my translucent cup
To prepare the tea and savor it in solitude.
The first cup moistened my lips and throat,
The second banished my loneliness.
The third lifted the heaviness that oppressed my mind from
so much study.
The fourth brought a light perspiration that dispersed through
my pores all of life's afflictions.
The fifth purified me.
The sixth opened the kingdom of the Immortals to me.
The seventh—ah, would that I could drink more!
I perceived nothing more than the soft breath of wind that
swelled my sleeves.
Transported by that sweet breeze, I attained the heavens.

Above: Reproduction of an antique Chinese teapot made of Yixing clay. Private collection.

We do not know if Lu Tung's poetry crossed the sea, as did that of Saicho, a Japanese Buddhist monk who introduced tea to his own country at the very beginning of the ninth century. Chinese culture influenced the entire Far East at the time, and Saicho was one of the many Buddhist monks who traveled to China to study its writing, religion and politics. The monks brought back the precious leaves from their travels and established the first tea plantations around their monasteries. It was not until the thirteenth century that tea descended from its seclusion in these meditative retreats and appeared on the tables of noblemen and samurai.

Below: Bamboo whisks, used for the *Cha No Yu* tea ceremony, first appeared in the Song dynasty.

From powder to infused tea

During China's Song dynasty (960–1279), tea leaves were ground into a green powder in a stone mill and whipped in water with a small bamboo whisk. This method of preparation is the origin of the *Cha No Yu* (Japanese tea ceremony), which is practiced even today in Japan.

Above: Cultivating and drying
China green tea in the
nineteenth century.
Engraving by George
Newenham Wright, 1843,
private collection.

Tea was not infused as we prepare it today until the Ming dynasty
(1368–1644). Westerners discovered the infused beverage in the seventeenth
century. To control the already flourishing tea trade, the Chinese government
opened a Bureau of Tea and Horses, a testament to the vital role played by tea
in the Chinese economy. The bureau oversaw the barter of tea for horses with
tribal people on the frontiers. Meanwhile, ceramists refined their art, creating
new cups, with handles and without, and even kettles.

Between 1644 and 1911, China was ruled by the Qing dynasty, which abol-
ished the duty on tea. This decision demonstrates how the precious leaves
had become an absolute necessity, a staple like rice and salt, which were also
exempt from taxes. The most popular types of tea at that time were green tea,
black tea and blue-green oolong.

Tea conquers the west

Transporting sacks of tea on a plantation in Ceylon. Lipton, like many other companies that emerged between the middle and the end of the nineteenth century, built a large empire based on tea.

Tea had already reached the West well before the seventeenth century. There is an allusion to it as early as 851 in a manuscript composed by Sulayman, an Arab trader, who described tea as "an herb which has more leaves than a clover and a bit more fragrance as well, although it is very bitter. You boil water and pour the leaves on top." His lack of enthusiasm was shared by Marco Polo (1254–1324), who declared in his *Description of the Marvels of the World* that this "exotic" drink was best reserved for women and the elderly. Tea had to bide its time for several centuries longer before conquering the West.

Europe discovers tea

Holland's Dutch East India Company traders imported the first cases of tea to Europe by sea around 1606. The tea was bartered for sage.

Before the end of the first half of the seventeenth century, tea had reached London, Paris and Amsterdam, but its high price restricted the availability to the nobility and wealthy middle class. The tea trade was initially controlled by the Dutch, but the English began to compete in 1699. To gain control of the tea and spice trade, the British East India Company launched a political offensive that resulted in their monopoly over transactions with China from 1715 to 1834.

The English very quickly developed a passion for the beverage. England had numerous trading hubs, with Madras, Calcutta and Bombay among the most important. Tea was consumed in the cafés of these business centers by the middle of the century. In 1657, Thomas Galloway established a tea company and organized auctions on his premises. Soon thereafter, Charles II ascended the throne (1660-1685). His Portuguese wife, Catherine of Braganza, brought the Indian city of Bombay as part of her dowry. She relished tea, drinking it in copious quantities, and introduced the custom of "tea time" to the court, a practice that endures to this day. Tea also made its conquest of the ruling classes in France beginning in 1636. It was originally consumed for medicinal purposes and sold by apothecaries along with tisanes and other remedies. Cardinal Mazarin (1602–1661) was a great tea drinker and enthusiast, convinced that tea was an effective remedy for his gout. King Louis XIV himself enjoyed it for its digestive properties.

Tea was regarded as medicinal, but that perception did not prevent consumers from taking an interest in enhancing their enjoyment of its flavor. Tea drinkers began to add milk to the beverage. During the reign of the Sun King, Madame de la Sablière found she could preserve the whiteness of her delicate porcelain by pouring a bit of cold milk into the bottom of her treasured cups before adding the tea.

As we all know, the finest recipes are often discovered by chance. The Englishman Lord Grey (1764–1845) had received exotic bergamot as a gift. As he sipped his tea, he examined the fruit and sliced into it. He added a bit to his cup and found the result delicious. Ever since, one of the best loved and widely enjoyed teas remains Earl Grey, a tea scented with bergamot.

The end of a monopoly

Far from the comfortable manor house of that ingenious aristocrat, English colonists who had settled on the east coast of North America were dependent on trade with their mother country, which was also the source of all their vital supplies. When the king of England raised duties and taxes on tea in 1767, the colonists protested. The discontent of these British subjects mounted until 1773, when a revolutionary movement against British tyranny was organized. On December 16, the infuriated colonists tossed overboard more than 300 cases of tea that had been transported in large ships anchored in Boston harbor. The "Boston Tea Party" was the first step toward independence for the future United States of America.

Less than a hundred years later, tea provided yet another opportunity for Americans to defy the English. In the mid-nineteenth century, private American companies, taking advantage of the end of the British East India Company's monopoly, launched tea clippers. These elegant ships with slim, streamlined hulls and impressive sails surpassed all earlier speed records,

Below: The Dutch were the first to import tea to Europe, around 1606. Dutch squadron from the India Company. Painting by Backuysen Ludolf, seventeenth century, Louvre Museum.

charting swift courses to distant oceans and competing with each other to be the first to reach London with their precious cargoes of spices and tea.

Along with China, one of the clippers' favored destinations was India, among the primary producers of "English Tea" until its independence in 1947. The Assam Company had been established in 1839 to facilitate trade of Indian teas. The province of Assam produced particularly robust black teas, still admired today for their distinctive flavor, which is enhanced by a splash of milk.

The era of large tea companies

More interested in China than in India, the noted botanist Robert Fortune embarked on a fabulous voyage in 1845. Disguised as a Mandarin, he traveled all over the country with a guide, visiting tea-growing regions. He brought back several varieties of tea from this first expedition that were sent to the Himalayas, where their cultivation failed. Determined and convinced that the climate of India, and particularly that of Darjeeling, was well suited to the cultivation of Camellia sinensis, Fortune undertook another expedition. After numerous thwarted attempts, he managed to get the imported seeds to grow in tiny greenhouses. Fortune's project succeeded, and the gardens of Darjeeling, which have produced some of the world's most celebrated tea since 1850, are a testimony to his triumph.

Above: Sir Thomas Lipton was certainly one of the most famous of the great tea adventurers. Today his name is permanently associated with Ceylon tea.

Thomas Lipton was born in Glasgow in the same year of 1850. The son of Irish immigrants, he left for America, where he tried his hand at various modest trades. He soon became homesick, however, and returned to the old country, where he used his small savings to set up shop in his native city in 1871. He was an innovator, using advertising to promote his business, and quickly achieved a good reputation. After this initial success, he established himself in London in 1894. Fascinated by tea, he purchased plantations in Ceylon. "From the plantation to your table with no middleman" was the slogan that made his fortune. He was knighted in 1902, becoming Sir Thomas Lipton.

Other universally recognized British brands of tea include Twinings and Fortnum and Mason. At the beginning of the nineteenth century, these companies started to buy tea from Ceylon. The Dutch had been the first to occupy this island, particularly the region of Colombo, in the seventeenth and eighteenth centuries. There had been magnificent coffee plantations there until the invasion of a pernicious fungus devastated them. Tea was introduced

Left: A China tea plantation in the Botanical Garden of Rio de Janeiro in the nineteenth century. During this century, tea plants had been introduced to many regions of the globe. Print by Léon-Jean-Baptiste Sabatier and Victor Adam, 1835, Royal Geographical Society, London.

as a replacement crop in 1834. Ever since, Sri Lanka has been one of the world's most important tea producers and exporters. These days, its plantations no longer belong to the British, who have also been stripped of their exclusivity in the traditions of tea time, breakfast tea, five o'clock tea, tea for you, tea for two, and the tea cozy!

England's national drink

Today the British consume more than 6.6 lbs. of tea per capita annually, as compared to 3/4 lb. for Americans and 1/2 lb. for the French. Tea does indeed remain Britain's national beverage, even if the European trade is now handled through Hamburg rather than London. The consumption of tea in France stood at only 1/4 lb. per capita annually in the 1980s, but it has been steadily on the rise since then. There are numerous tea shops and salons scattered throughout France's larger cities. The first Salon International du Thè was held in Paris in 2000. This gathering was a great success, buoyed by a widespread public perception that tea is beneficial to health.

Right: Wooden tea chests from Sri Lanka, holding about 66 lbs. These chests are ideal for transporting and storing tea, but are often replaced today by more economical cloth or paper sacks.

The passion for tea spread to many other countries throughout the world. In Russia, for example, the Chinese ambassador introduced tea in 1618 when he presented it as a gift to Czar Alexis in Moscow. As in England and France, the beverage became ubiquitous at the court and soon captivated the entire nation. A century later, people in the Urals crafted the first samovars that were used to prepare highly concentrated tea, "tea liquor." Water was maintained at a boil in a receptacle kept over hot coals all day long. A small amount of the "tea liquor" was drawn into a glass and water poured on top. Russians sipped their tea, while dissolving a little lump of sugar in their mouths. In this land

where winters are so severe, the practice continues to this day. While the samovars may be electric today, this sweetened beverage still offers comforting warmth to tea lovers.

Russia is a tea-producing nation, although its cultivation and production have been disorganized and limited since the dissolution of the USSR. Nevertheless, Russians still consume about 1.3 lbs. of tea per capita annually. Those with the means to do so select varieties from the great plantations, especially Darjeeling.

Tea was also introduced to Germany in the seventeenth century, generally through apothecaries, as in France. A Royal Tea Company, responsible for importing tea directly from China, was established in 1752. Germans gradually acquired the habit of tea consumption, and today they purchase 5/8 lb. of tea per capita annually. Like the English, they often drink tea with a splash of milk or a little cream.

These levels of consumption pale compared to that of Morocco, which enthusiastically goes through 2.2 lbs. per capita annually. The English introduced tea to Morocco in the middle of the nineteenth century when they were seeking new markets. At that time, Moroccans drank infusions of mint. Tea was an immediate hit in Morocco, but did not detract from the people's love of their mint infusions, which continued unabated. A blend of the two beverages became Morocco's national drink, a symbol of hospitality. Today, no Moroccan household would receive a guest without offering mint tea. Morocco and the other North African countries use exclusively China green tea known as gunpowder, with fresh mint and sugar. An authentic tea ceremony, rich in symbolism and charm, endures in these countries.

Tea is the most popular drink in the world today after water. A refined and diversified life-style has developed around it. Right: Tuo Cha tea next to a Japanese tea set. Below: A porcelain teacup reproduced by the long-established Royal Bernardaud company. An indispensable "tea time" accessory.

Along the Green Tree Trail

The tea plant

Left: Cultivated tea plants.
They are generally pruned
to a height varying between
3 and 5 ft. Left untouched,
the tea plant can easily
reach 50 ft. in height.

Tea is the most popular beverage, after water, in the world today. The leaves used for this highly appreciated infusion are taken from the shrub called Camellia sinensis or Thea sinensis by botanists. As the Latin name suggests, the tea plant is an illustrious member of the camellia family, which includes a little over 80 species. The evergreen leaves, from 1 1/4 to 7 3/4 in. long, may be smooth, stiff, dull or shiny, depending on the variety. It is rare to see the white blossoms in the plantations: the harvest begins with the buds, pekoe or young shoots, prized by connoisseurs.

Growing conditions for the tea plant

Certain tea plants have adapted to cool regions, to plantations in high altitudes and even to relatively dry conditions, while others flourish in hot, humid climates, with volcanic soil. Ideally, the soil should contain neither clay nor calcium, and should instead be acidic and loose, abundant in potassium, nitrogen, and phosphoric acid. With respect to the climate, it is best if the temperature is not too hot, ranging from 50 to 86°F, with five hours of sun per day, cool nights, dry and regular winds, and frequent rainfall (between 8 and 10 ft. per year) at night. A favorable humidity level ranges between 70 and 90 percent.

In the wild, the tea plant can reach 33 to 50 ft. in height and up to 100 ft. for some rare specimens that are several hundred years old. However, on the plantations they are pruned to between 3 and 5 ft. to facilitate plucking. Tea plants can be grown from seeds, or plant cuttings although professionals today favor growing bushes from cuttings.

27

Left: *Camellia sinensis*, one of the 80 species of the camellia family. Etching by Dr. Woodville, 1794, private collection, London.

For nine months, the young bushes are cared for attentively, nurtured in nurseries dedicated to their cultivation. The tea plants must grow for another five or six years before they can be plucked to generate revenues for the plantation. This is a relatively short time given the length of the plant's life, which ranges from 30 to 50 years for Indian varieties, and more than 100 years for Chinese varieties. In addition to the type of tea plant, the quality of the pluckings depends on the care given by the plantation. Men are usually in charge, whereas plucking is traditionally women's work.

The plucking and the processing of the leaves results in a white, green, blue-green, black, roasted or smoked tea, though they all come from the same bush! It is the method used for drying the leaves after they are plucked that generates different drinks.

Right: Tea leaves from a plantation in Sri Lanka: smooth and shiny, they are used for manufacturing black tea.

Tea harvesting and manufacture

Only the bud leaf and the top leaves—between one and four, depending on the quality of the tea processed—are plucked from the plant.
Left: A Sri Lankan plucker.

The first European botanists believed that black teas and green teas came from two different types of tea plants; in fact, all teas are derived from the same plant. The differences in the teas arise from geographic and climactic factors, in addition to the harvesting and processing of the leaves

The harvesting

The harvesting period generally lasts for about eight months, from March to the end of September or the beginning of October. The tea leaves are most often plucked by hand, although machines are also used.

The sap is concentrated in the bud leaves, so the leaves closest to the bud leaf are the best quality. Except in Africa, women traditionally pluck the tea leaves, relying on their slender hands and their dexterity, as well as their endurance, to complete the task. Working in scorching weather, they repeat the same motion 50,000 times daily from dawn to dusk. Each plucker must carry a basket strapped to her back that contains up to 66 lbs. of leaves. After the manufacturing process, just 15.5 lbs. of tea remain.

Mechanical or semi-mechanical plucking can take place only in plain areas. The leaves are cut and vacuumed into baskets. In Japan, leaves plucked in this manner are reserved for the roasted green teas such as Bancha Hojicha, which is considered a "classical plucking."

There are three types of pluckings, depending on the quality of the tea desired: "imperial plucking", "fine plucking", and "classical plucking."
• For "imperial plucking," only the bud leaf and top first leaf are picked. The

bud leaf, or pekoe, with its white down, is actually the tip of a fresh branch surrounded by an undeveloped young leaf. In China, this plucking was reserved for the emperor. There was a time when only young virgins wearing white gloves gathered the leaves. This ritual has disappeared today, along with the use of trained monkeys to pick the leaves of unpruned tea plants out of human reach. White tea is made from plucking only the top bud.

• "Fine plucking" is the most common method. Here, the bud leaf and two top leaves are picked. This method is reserved for teas of good or superior quality.

• "Classic plucking" includes three or four top leaves along with the bud leaf. It is reserved for roasted or smoked teas.

The harvesting of tea leaves in the Ootacamund region of India (above), and in Japan, near Tokyo (right). In most tea-growing countries, plucking by hand is women's work.

The manufacture of tea

White, green, blue-green, black, roasted and smoked teas come from the same plant; it is the processing of the leaves that makes the difference. Manufacturing facilities must be located in very close proximity to the plantations, as the tea leaves become damaged and withered in less than 36 hours.

Black tea

Black tea is usually called "red tea" by the Chinese. It is tea that has been fermented. The most common method is the "orthodox" process during which the tea undergoes six operations: withering, rolling, roll breaking, fermentation, firing, and sifting. Black tea produces a copper-colored infusion.

• Withering, which can be performed manually or mechanically, takes place immediately after the harvest and makes the leaves more pliable for rolling.

32

The leaves are arranged on ventilated wicker racks to dry. They lose 50 percent of their moisture during this operation. Manual wilting takes from 16 to 24 hours, while the mechanized procedure is completed in six hours. The accelerated method improves profitability while guaranteeing more uniform withering.

• Traditionally, artisans rolled leaves by hand. Today, the leaves are often processed by machines called "rollers." For a half hour the leaves are rolled over each other, allowing the cells from broken leaves to release oils and juices that spur fermentation.

• During the roll-breaking phase, leaves pass through a sorting belt. The first pass-through extracts the least broken leaves. In subsequent pass-throughs, the leaves are sorted according to size. This operation also allows them to cool down.

• Fermentation is the most delicate of the operations and the most important for black tea. This phase of the tea transformation process takes one to three hours. It requires the knowledge of an expert, a master of fermentation. The leaves are placed in a humid environment, at a temperature of 72 to 82°F, where they slowly oxidize. The absorption of oxygen gives them a hue ranging from tawny to black depending on the quantity of chlorophyll present.

Double previous page: At the end of the day, the pluckers from the region of Nuwara Eliya, Sri Lanka, wait for their tea harvest to be transported to the processing plant.

Left: Tea plucking in the Shizuka region in Japan. These tea leaves will be used for preparing Bancha Hojicha.

36

Right: tea is then weighed and the pluckers are paid based on the weight of their harvest.

• The drying or pan-firing stage stops fermentation. For twenty minutes, the leaves are placed in a chamber of dry air where the temperature ranges from 194 to 203°F. The tea leaves are then cooled and spread out on large trays. The blackened leaves contain no more than five percent moisture at most.

• During the sifting process, the leaves are sorted and placed in three categories: leaf grade, broken grade, and fannings or dust. This classification does not indicate the quality of the tea, but rather the strength. The more broken the leaves, the stronger the infusion they produce.

Smoked black tea

Large mature souchong leaves, rolled lengthwise, are used to obtain smoked black tea. The process is identical to that used for black tea, except that the leaves are placed on hot iron trays only after fermentation, where they are

lightly roasted. They are then spread on bamboo racks or baskets and held above a fire of pine or cypress wood. The smoke permeates the leaves, resulting in a tea that varies in its degree of smokiness, depending on the length of the process.

Great Wall of China, a lightly smoked tea, is considered among the best of this type, while Lapsang Souchong, the best known and most popular, is a medium smoked variety and Tarry Souchong is the smokiest variety.

These teas, which are often simply called "Chinese teas," are produced only in China for a relatively small audience given the large size of the country's production.

Blue-green tea

Blue-green Oolong or Wulong (Black Dragon) tea is a semi-fermented tea that originated in China and Formosa. In recent years, attempts have been made to produce it in India, especially in Darjeeling with its Garden of Gopaldhara variety, but this market is still marginal.

To obtain this blue-green tea, the leaves undergo partial fermentation: from 12 to 20 percent of the fermentation time for black tea in China, and 60 to 70 percent of the fermentation time in Taiwan. The leaves, which are delicately

Several steps in the processing of Ceylon tea: drying, fermenting on racks, sorting to extract the least broken leaves and packing in wooden crates. The crates specify the name of the plantation, the garden, the leaf grade (B.O.P. here), the packing date and the weight.

38

manipulated by hand, remain whole. They produce a deep yellow or orange drink, low in caffeine. These light teas can be consumed at day's end, especially Formosa Black Dragon, a magnificent tea with a hint of chestnuts.

Green tea

Green tea is not fermented; it simply undergoes one of two different firing methods.

In China, the plucked tea is dried at a very high temperature (212°F) in copper or iron pans placed over a fire for a brief period of time sufficient to deactivate the leaf enzymes and thereby prevent their fermentation. After they are rolled and dried, the leaves pass through a sifter. They are then sorted, rolled or flattened by hand again and any twigs are removed.

In Japan, the drying process is accomplished by steaming the leaves at about 176°F. This method is more mechanized. The leaves are then rolled, dried and sifted in the Chinese manner, but the sorting operation is conducted mechanically. The green tea infusion is yellow in color. Included in this category are the wonderful Chinese Lung Ching (Dragon Well) and the Japanese Gyokuro. To prepare a proper cup of Gyokuro, the water temperature must not exceed 140°F, and the steeping time should range from 45 seconds to one minute.

White tea

White tea has been produced exclusively in China since the beginning of the Song dynasty (960–1279). The buds (pekoe) are carefully spread out, sorted, and dried. The tea leaves undergo only two operations: withering, followed immediately by drying under the sun, in a pan, or by steam. This tea makes a very pale yellow liquor, and is prepared by steeping in water not to exceed 167°F for seven to 20 minutes according to taste. It can withstand several infusions.

Yin Zhen (Silver Needle), Pai Mu Tan (White Peony) and Pai Hao Yin are among the rare teas originating in the Chinese province of Fujian, along with Happy Country.

Packing

Tea is packed in wooden chests, which are highly prized today, or in thick sacks marked with the name of the country of origin, plantation, tea garden, and the packaging date. It is then shipped off for sampling around the world.

Classification and grade

Tea productions are sorted by grades, with categories that pertain mostly to the appearance of the leaves and their quality. These universal classifications give valuable information regarding the choice of teas.

Above: Drying and sifting, two steps in the processing of China green tea.

Right: An exceptionally beautiful package of small wooden crates weighing 2.2 lbs. from India.

Classification of fermented black teas

There are four major families of black tea: Orange Pekoe (O.P.), Flowery Orange Pekoe (F.O.P.), Souchong and Pekoe (P.), referring to leaves edged with a bit of downy white. Souchong includes the largest lower leaves and is reserved for smoked tea in China.

Other names provide the consumer with information regarding certain of the tea's characteristics.

- Tip refers to the extreme tip of the bud, used for very high-quality teas.
- Orange designates a "royal" tea, of superior quality.
- Flowery indicates the tea is flavored with buds containing juice.
- If there are numerous buds, the tea is considered a Golden variety.
- Broken indicates that the tea contains broken or cut leaves.
- S.F. designates special fine leaves, a plucking of exceptional quality.

These designations may be combined as follows:
- When buying an O.P. or Orange Pekoe, the consumer enjoys the taste of a superior quality tea which contains buds and two top leaves.
- A B.O.P. or Broken Orange Pekoe offers superior quality with buds and broken leaves giving a drink that has a redder hue and a more robust flavor.
- A G.F.O.P. or Golden Flowery Orange Pekoe designates a tea of superior quality with first leaves and buds.

The finest tea would be designated S.F.T.G.F.O.P. or Super Fine Tippy Golden Flowery Orange Pekoe. By contrast, the B.P. or Broken Pekoe includes second and third broken leaves, and is reserved for blends.

Classification of broken leaf teas

The following classifications are used to describe broken leaf teas:
- Fannings include small finely broken leaves that provide very full-bodied teas with good color. The well-known fannings called Saint James of Ceylon is especially strong: 1/2 tsp. is sufficient for six cups.
- Dust designates a small broken leaf, often smaller than 1/16 in., that is reserved for tea bags.

Classification of green teas

The classification of green teas is much simpler. It includes:
- Gunpowder, which is shaped into small pellets made from rolled leaves, is used alone or may be flavored with mint, for example.

Gunpowder China green tea
in a Chinese measuring spoon
of Yixing clay.

• Chunmee leaves are rolled lengthwise.
• Natural Leaf is a tea made from flat whole leaves.
• Matcha designates a variety of leaf that is ground into powder in a stone mill. One of the most famous comes from the Gyokuro garden in Japan and is used for the tea ceremony.

Classification of blue-green teas

Blue-green teas are classified in grades ranging from Extra Choicest to Dust and Fannings, depending on the quality and taste of the tea.

Classification of white teas

White teas are not graded, since they include only the buds.

A professional, seeking to meet the desires of his clientele, will find that these various classifications provide valuable assistance. The tea connoisseur, looking for the best service from a tea shop, is therefore advised to specify the times of day when he prefers to drink his tea as well as his taste preferences (strong or weak, with or without milk).

A trip around the world

A tea plantation near Tokyo,
Japan. The Japanese
produce only green tea.
All the black tea they
consume is thus imported.

While China, India, Sri Lanka, and Kenya have together accounted for two-thirds of the world's tea production since 1929, plantations flourish today in over forty countries including Taiwan, Japan, Korea, Thailand, Vietnam, Laos, Burma, Russia, Iran, Turkey, Argentina, Brazil, Cameroon, Zimbabwe, Mauritius, and Réunion. The plant has adapted to many continents, with the exception of Europe.

China

China manufactures 700,000 tons of tea annually. It is the oldest exporter of tea in the world and the second largest in terms of volume. It has eight major tea-producing regions: Yunnan, Anhui, Fujian, Zhejiang, Guangxi, Sichuan, Guangdon, and Hunan.

The Chinese claim that it takes more than a lifetime to sample and discover all the tea from the country's gardens, and it is true that every type of tea is produced in China. Its plantations represent more than half the total area of tea plantations in Asia. However, profitability is lower than in other countries, as handmade methods are still used.

The Chinese consume 80 percent of the green tea they produce and export the major portion of their black tea. Production and distribution are controlled by a state monopoly, although each region is responsible for its own activities. Each province is allowed a scheduled harvest of of tea that must be constant in quality.

High-altitude plantations flourish under the mist, and benefit from regular rainfall that guarantees an ideal level of humidity for the processing and manufacture of tea.

China white teas

In the southeast, the province of Fujian produces a diverse range of teas. The white teas are harvested in this special region. There are three particularly renowned varieties:

• Yin Zhen (Silver Needle), a mythical white tea composed of silvery buds, comes from the imperial plucking, It was used to pay imperial tributes during the Qing dynasty, and even under the Tang and Song dynasties, according to certain historians. This tea, with silvery leaves covered in a white down, is rare and highly esteemed, and boasts a fresh, subtle aroma. As with all white teas, it undergoes no fermentation. The buds are roasted at 90°F and then wrapped in paper and stored for two days in wooden cases. They undergo a second roasting at lower temperatures and are wrapped and held for one more day before their final roasting.

A product of the Shui Hsien and Dai Bai (Great White) tea plants, this tea comes primarily from the regions of Jianyang (Fujian) and Jun Shan (Mount Hunan). Rich in vitamin C, it has a flowery, sweet flavor. It should be prepared with water at 140 or 158°F and infused four to fifteen minutes.

• Pai Mu Tan or Bai Mu Dan (White Peony) includes several silvery buds along with the top two whole leaves plucked in the spring harvest. The branch looks like a flower and the leaves are covered in abundant white down. This very fine white tea emits a delicate, mellow aroma after it is infused for four to 20 minutes in water at 158 to 176°F.

• Yun Cha (Tea of Clouds) from Yunnan is esteemed for its exceptional quality. With classic white tea flavor, the infusion is luminous. It is steeped for two or three minutes at a temperature of 158°F.

China green teas

• The province of Anhui, West of Shanghai, produces primarily Chun Mee (Old Man's Eyebrow), a whole leaf green tea rolled lengthwise. Its liquor is fine and well developed, and its aroma is pure, powerful, and persistent.

- Ding Gu Da Fang emits a flowery aroma spiked with the light taste of chestnuts. Ideally it should be prepared with water at 158°F and infused for two quick minutes.

- Taiping Houkui has the delicate taste of orchids. It is a wonderful high-altitude tea that should be prepared with water at 158°F and infused for three to four minutes.

- Mao Feng, certainly the most famous China green, is plucked from the celebrated Jiu Hua mountain. Its mellow smelling liquor is sweet with burnt overtones. The tea should be steeped at 158°F for three minutes before drinking.

Above: A tea plucker on a plantation in the region of Hangzhou.

Right: Lung Ching tea (Dragon Well). Once infused, the leaves turn pale green.

- Huo Qiang is rolled by hand into grayish green pearls and produces a mellow infusion. It is an expensive top quality tea, prized by connoisseurs, who savor it at a temperature of 158°F. It can withstand several successive infusions.

- Huo Shan Huang, from Yellow Mountain, boasting very fine and long greenish yellow needles, is particularly refreshing.

- The famous Huang Shan Mao Feng is a sculpted green tea. Its leaves are joined by hand, then attached to each other to form a pompom of 200 buds and top leaves. Its graceful bouquet can be enjoyed throughout the day in a zhong, a Chinese covered cup. Watching the dance of the infused leaves adds greatly to the pleasure of the tea.

• Hunan is distinguished for its production of "yellow" or golden green teas, including the mysterious tea of the Five Dynasties, one of the most famous and rare Chinese teas. Less mythical, Mao Jian is a tea grown in the high mountains with long, fine, and down-covered leaves. It provides an aromatic cup that is pure and very fruity, but delicate in flavor.

• In the province of Jiangsu, the most highly regarded and exceptional tea is without doubt the Pi Lo Chun (Spring Spiral Jade). Made of buds and the top two leaves, it is extremely refined. Round in body, it is greenish in hue, with a combined flowery and fruity taste. It is an exceptional tea that should be steeped at 158°F for one to two minutes before tasting.

"Sculpted teas"—where the leaves are joined and attached by hand—can withstand several infusions. Over the course of these infusions, the tea loses some intensity of flavor, but its delicacy remains. Ju Hua Cha China green tea (above) and Jade Needle (right) before and after infusion.

• The Zhejiang is a beautiful region south of Jiangsu. It specializes in flat or rolled leaf green tea.

- The famous Gunpowder, with its leaves shaped into balls or pearls is frequently used, in Morocco especially, to prepare green mint tea. This tea will appeal to those who prefer a full-bodied taste, especially when the tea is drunk alone.

- Chun Mee (Old Man's Eyebrow) is another brilliant green tea, strong and full bodied.

- The famous Lung Ching (Dragon Well) grows on the summit of the Tieh Mu Mountains. The flat leaves generate a vigorous and vitamin-rich infusion that is a lovely light green, the color of jade, with an exquisite aroma.

- Pei Hou is the crown jewel of the region, a rare garden prized for the golden green tender leaves it grows at the top of the mountain. It takes five hours on foot to reach the plantations where the precious leaves are plucked by hand in the traditional ancestral manner. Each plucker gathers only one kilo of tea per day. Men carry the loaded tea chests down the mountain on their backs.

• The province of Jiang Xi, located West of Fujian, produces a green tea with a silvery tone called the Emperor's Tea, as it was the choice of the imperial family since the third century.

• The province of Hubei is famous for its tea bricks, and for the Xia Zhou Bi Feng, a clear green tea, very fresh and smooth in taste.

• The mellow Douyun Mao Jiang (Silver Hook or Snowflakes) is found in the provinces of Guangxi and Guizhou along with the fine, delicate White Downy, a green tea that is sometimes incorrectly called a white tea because of its white downy leaves.

China blue-green teas

The Chinese also prepare blue-green or semi-fermented teas called Oolongs, which usually come from the Fujian province. Ti Kuan Yin (Iron Goddess of Mercy) is legendary for its beautiful dark leaves and its delicate flowery flavor. Shui Hsein (Water Fairies) is mellow and lightly spicy.

The province of Guangdon also produces Oolongs. Its most famous garden is called Feng Huang Dan Gong, known for its long twisted leaves. This tea, with its robust aroma, is perfect for evenings. The region of Yunnan houses the beautiful garden of Shen Xian, whose tea can withstand several infusions of fifteen seconds in water at 203°F

These semi-fermented teas are used for Gong Fu Cha, the Chinese ceremonial tea.

China black teas

Black teas made primarily for export represent about 20 percent of Chinese production. They are classified into three major categories: classic, smoked and flavored.

• Classic black teas

The teas from the province of Yunnan are well-known in France, under various names such as Yunnan, Yunnan Imperial and Grand Yunnan. They are sometimes called "tea mochas." The high-altitude plantations provide some of the best brews in China, with a well-rounded and mellow fragrance, pleasant to drink at any time of day. Pu Erh also comes from this region, and is often used to make Tuo Cha tea, which is compressed into the shape of a nest. It is sold as loose tea in certain tea shops and salons de thé.

The liquor is very dark red and has a unique damp, earthy taste. As it is low in caffeine, it can be drunk throughout the day and enjoyed for its diuretic and medicinal benefits, which have been recognized for centuries.

In addition to the green teas, the province of Anhui also offers excellent quality black teas including Keemun, made of beautiful even and short leaves with a delicate taste. Low in caffeine, it is a perfect evening tea. The infusion is red. Plantations in the province of Sichuan, located at an altitude of more than 5,000 ft., produce teas with a subtle liquor distinguished by the presence of several tips.

A China tea plantation in the region of Hangzhou, the ancient imperial capital and one of the most prosperous cities in the country, known for its tea fields.

• Smoked black teas

The province of Fujian has produced a smoked black tea since the seventeenth century. This specialty was invented by chance: to resolve the problem of a delayed delivery, a manufacturer lit a fire from pine wood to speed up the drying process. The leaves were permeated by the smoke, and a new taste was born.

The most famous of these teas is Lapsang Souchong, a medium-smoked variety, and Tarry Souchong, the smokiest variety.

Yin Zhen (Silver Needle) China green tea before and after infusion

• Flavored black teas

The Chinese have always flavored certain teas with jasmine, orchids, chrysanthemums, and lotus flowers.

India

Producing about 900,000 tons per year, India is the largest grower of tea in the world. Three regions contribute to this leading position, which the country has held since the beginning of the nineteenth century: Darjeeling, Assam, and Nilgiri. Indian teas are generally not used to create flavored teas. In the northeast, in the Himalayan foothills, the 85 Darjeeling gardens are dedicated to high-altitude black teas. Their exceptional quality has earned the title "champagne of teas." The first flush Darjeeling Gopaldhara, the Singbulli, and the Balasun are exceptional.

For several years, the province of Darjeeling has also produced blue-green teas (semi-fermented or Oolong) such as the Garden of Gopaldhara. These delicious teas are made in very small quantities and command high prices in specialty tea shops.

Assam, a region of plains in northeast India, produces robust, quite full-bodied black teas, enhanced by a splash of milk. Organic Assam Berjan is a dark green tea with a light tone of spruce. Assam teas are often used in making blends such as Breakfast Tea, sharing their character with Ceylon teas. They also stand alone.

Nilgri, a mountain region in the south of India, produces high-quality teas that are still not well known in France.

A feature of Indian tea

India is the only country that produces teas where quality is associated with the time of plucking. Importers around the world wait each year for the first flush. It begins in March and is over at the end of April, producing a black tea with a delicate muscat or green almond flavor, highly prized by connoisseurs. Darjeeling of this growth should be drunk plain after the leaves are infused for two to three minutes in water at 185°F.

The in-between flush takes place between the end of April and the end of May. With a slightly more mature taste, the liquor retains much of the freshness of the first flush.

The summer harvest (second flush) occurs between May and July and produces well-rounded teas with a more mature fruit taste. The optimum

53

flavor is achieved when the water is 185°F and the tea is infused for four to five minutes.

A final autumn flush occurs on certain plantations from the beginning of October to the end of November. The leaves are larger, their taste stronger and their color redder.

Ceylon

Although Ceylon became Sri Lanka in May 1972, its teas are still sold as "Ceylon tea."

With its 300,000 tons, this island, the site of the plantations of Sir Thomas Lipton, is the third-largest producer and the largest exporter in the world today. The hot and humid climate is ideal for cultivating tea plants that yield primarily black tea. The English have maintained their preference for this rather full-bodied tea, drinking it with a splash of milk.

The pluckings are categorized according to the altitude of the plantation: High Grown for the best gardens located at altitudes between 4,000 and 8,000 ft.; Middle Grown for those located between 2,000 and 4,000 ft.; and Low Grown for the lower zones. Six regions are known for their tea: Kandy, at a lower altitude, Galle, in the south of the island, Ratnapura, close to Colombo, Dimbula, Nuvara Eliya, and Uva.

Above: In high-altitude Nilgiri, India, the tea plantations grow at an altitude of up to 6,500 ft.

Right: Along with black teas, India also produces several blue-green teas such as this Darjeeling Oolong.

54

Above: A tea plantation in Kenya. The English introduced the first tea plants in 1925, in regions where rice paddies already existed.

Double previous page and left: The Nuvara Eliya region has the most beautiful tea fields in Sri Lanka.

The gardens of Pettiagalla, Keniworth, and Dimbula are in Dimbula, located at 4,100 ft. and producing very full-bodied teas of good quality.

At 6,500 ft., Nuvara Eliya has the reputation of being one of the finer growths in Ceylon.

In the southeast, Saint James and Uva Highland foster the Uva region's good reputation with their very high quality teas.

Ceylon teas are always used in breakfast tea blends. They yield a dark and full-bodied infusion.

Kenya

Kenya is the fourth largest tea producer in the world with 280,000 tons, despite the fact that the first plantations were not established until 1925. It is the largest producer on the African continent. Kenya manufactures only black teas, including the tasty Marinyn with gold-tipped, uniform leaves. Unlike the Asian countries, which consume the majority of their production, African countries drink small quantities of tea and export the vast majority.

Turkey

Turkey is the fifth largest producer in the world with 180,000 tons of primarily black tea. Near the Black Sea, the province of Rize generates a very mellow fine leaf tea. The country's export volume is relatively low, since local consumption is significant.

Japan

A country with a great tea tradition, Japan is the sixth largest producer of tea in the world with 85,000 tons annually of green tea and roasted green tea. The Japanese are major consumers of tea, which they use generously for drinks, ice cream (flavored with Matcha), noodles and other products. Their tea plantations are superb and magnificently maintained, in the manner of the gardens of the Shizuoka and Uji regions, near Kyoto, at the base of Fuji-Yama where the famous Gyokuro is grown.

Gyokuro (Precious Rose) is a green tea especially rich in vitamin C that yields an emerald infusion with a unique taste. It should be prepared with water at 140°F and infused 45 to 60 seconds. Its regular, flat, dark green leaves, are plentiful in chlorophyll, as three weeks before the plucking season, the garden is covered with a black cloth. This procedure accelerates the movement of the sap to the bud, producing a tea that is ranked among the greatest growths in the world, precious, refined, and suitable for major occasions.

Matcha (Tea Powder) is obtained by grinding the Gyokuro leaves in a stone mill. Primarily intended for use in the tea ceremony, Cha No Yu is whipped with water using a bamboo whisk. The resulting pale green liquor is very thick, strong and concentrated. Recently, Matcha has been introduced in cooking. Sencha (Infused Tea) includes Sencha Yamato, a flat leaf green tea of exceptional quality that yields a very mellow tasting green infusion. There are several other high quality Japanese Senchas such as Ariake from the island of Kyushu, Kawanecha from Shizuoka, and Yame from the Fukoka region.

The splendid Japanese tea plantations are cut with circular saws, giving the tea plants their rounded shape.

Opposite: A tea field at the base of Fuji-Yama, in the Uji region.

Above: A box of blue-green Black Dragon tea, produced in Taiwan.

Left: The precious Japanese Matcha green tea is packaged in small metal boxes that contain no more than 1.5 oz.

Genmaicha is a flat leaf green tea that is mixed with popped corn and toasted rice kernels. Its unusual flavor makes it a good companion to a meal.

Bancha Hojicha is a large leaf roasted green tea, sometimes sold directly off barges in Tokyo by small local producers.

The Japanese are also very fond of imported black teas, especially those flavored with red fruit, rhubarb, mint or rose.

Taiwan (formerly Formosa)

The island of Taiwan has manufactured Oolong tea, blue-green, and semi-fermented, for many centuries. Today, its annual production is about 20,000 tons.

This mountainous island is well suited to the cultivation of tea, and the quality of its Oolong teas, which are semi-fermented (about 50 percent), attests to its reputation. These teas are darker, stronger, and fruitier than their Chinese counterparts.

Taiwan also produces flat leaf Senchas (often reserved for the Japanese market), rolled leaf Gunpowders and smoked black teas of an inferior quality to the Chinese and Japanese varieties.

The best-known gardens in Formosa include:

Dung Ding (Frozen Summit) from the mountain of the same name, is a delicious tea that produces a red infusion with light orange overtones and no bitter aftertaste.

Grand Pouchong is a beautiful, lightly fermented garden that produces a delicate tasting tea from its long, dark-colored and twisted leaves.

Ti Kuan Yin (Iron Goddess of Mercy), a famous plantation known for its semi-fermented tea (50 percent), is golden yellow in color and possesses a mellow, flowery taste.

Grand Oolong Fancy (Black Dragon) clearly outdoes the rest with its great aroma and subtle hint of chestnuts; it is a true marvel.

Green Tea as a Way of Life

Tea ceremonies

China, Japan and Morocco all use green tea for their tea ceremonies: green or blue-green tea in China, powdered green tea in Japan and green Gunpowder in Morocco.

Chung and *Gong Fu Cha* in China

The Chinese consume up to 20 cups of tea a day. The drink is carried to the office in the indispensable Thermos, and boiling water is regularly added to the leaves. Tea is prepared according to two different classical methods, *Chung* and *Gong Fu Cha*.

Chung or *Zhong*

In the *Chung* ceremony, tea is prepared in a handleless cup or wide-mouthed teacup, ideally white in color, equipped with a lid and a saucer. The lid symbolizes the heavens, the cup, man, and the saucer, the earth. This covered cup is used exclusively for green tea.

67

Left: Sculpted Tuo Cha black tea from the province of Yunnan, China, shaped into a small nest.

Right: Crimson glazed Chinese clay teapot, a reproduction of teapots used in the twelfth century during the Song dynasty.

Men use a slightly larger cup than women and hold it with two hands as a demonstration of their "deeply rooted" nature; women hold the cup with one hand. Gently moved aside, the lid holds back the leaves while the tea is sipped.

The tea leaves are placed in the bottom of the cup, moistened with a few drops of cold water and then covered in water at 158°F for two to three minutes before tasting. Certain teas can withstand several infusions during the day.

Gong Fu Cha

Less common than *Chung,* the *Gong Fu Cha* (Tea Time) ceremony has been practiced since the Ming dynasty (1368–1644). The teapot did not appear in China until the fifteenth century; before that time, the cauldron and ladle were the main tea utensils.

Gong Fu Cha is a symbol of welcome, hospitality, and sharing. It requires a serene setting and inspires the spirit to meditate. Over the centuries, this ceremony has been practiced in tea houses open only to men.

During the Cultural Revolution, Mao Tse-tung decided to close down tea houses, arguing that they impeded work. In reality, they sheltered poets, writers, and artists who represented a threat to his policies. These houses have reopened in recent years and even welcome women. They are decorated luxuriously with antique furniture that was probably hidden during the populist revolution. Tea ceremonies, and in particular Gong Fu Cha, are enhanced by the finest Yixing clay tea sets which are typically reserved for only one type of tea. The porous quality of the simple and unglazed teapots allows the aroma to diffuse freely.

Since the Ming period, only blue-green teas such as Ti Kuan Yin (Iron Goddess of Mercy) have been used for Gong Fu Cha service. The uten-

Above: Yu Huan (Jade Ring) China white tea in an enamel teacup with bamboo whisk (left), and infused in a porcelain teacup (right).

Right: China offers the largest variety of gardens in the world. Here are some of the Chinese sculpted teas.

70

Above: Lung Ching (Dragon Well) Chinese green tea.

Left: "Boat," Yixing clay teapot and cups, wooden spatula: many accessories are indispensable to the Chinese tea ceremony.

sils required for this meticulous preparation include a shallow tray with a reservoir called a "boat," a kettle, a clay teapot, and several small teacups, preferably made of clay, with white interiors. The dishes are warmed over the "boat." The warmed tea leaves are placed in the teapot and boiling water is added. The first infusion is thrown out. The operation is repeated, allowing the tea to infuse the second time around. As the teapots are small, the resulting tea is concentrated. This process is repeated three times.

To appreciate the sense of space and time of *Gong Fu Cha* in true serenity, the participant must drink the tea in small sips, breathe in the scent of the empty cup and allow the flavors to penetrate the back of the mouth.

Cha No Yu in Japan

The Buddhist monk Eisai, famous for having introduced Zen to Japan in the twelfth century, was the first to establish tea plants in the region of Uji, near Kyoto, which is the site of the greatest tea gardens in Japan today.

Tea's appeal spread slowly throughout the country. By the middle of the fifteenth century, Japanese monasteries had adopted the Sung rules of communal living from the Chinese, instituting in particular those governing the preparation and consumption of tea. The influence of the monks spread to warriors and feudal lords, whose meetings, called Chayoriai, took place over tea. These ceremonies evolved into *Cha No Yu*, the Way of Tea, which uses utensils originated in China. They were held in luxuriously decorated tea pavilions built by rich aristocrats who imported fine porcelain from China.

Murata Shuko (1422–1502) first laid down the rules of *Cha No Yu*. Tasting tea alone or in a small gathering, he sought moderation in the decoration of his tea house. Joining together in deep meditation, the master and his guests would drink the tea in small sips, slowly savoring this communion of the soul and the spirit. Through this ritual, Cha and Zen became intimately associated.

Above: A traditional paper-covered Japanese metal box containing green tea (left); a *Cha No Yu* accessory, a small fork used for serving pastries (right).

Right: Celadon teacup from Japan and Genmaicha Japanese green tea, mixed with toasted rice and popped corn.

Following double page: Accessories for the *Cha No Yu* ceremony: cast-iron teapot, bamboo whisk, spatula and ladle, stoneware dishes.

In the next century, Sen No Rikyu (1522–1591) introduced other more specific and formalized rules, raising *Cha No Yu* to its highest level of perfection and refinement.

Since the time of Rikyu, aspiring tea masters have undergone many years of training in schools that may vary in the rules they teach, but agree that the fundamentals of *Cha No Yu* are defined in terms of harmony, respect, purity, and serenity.

Cast-iron Japanese teapots with traditional bamboo ladle (above) and with Matcha (right). This tea is used today in making meals and sweets such as these green tea bonbons (below).

For the neophyte, the tea ceremony is an unforgettable experience, a voyage of initiation. Tea pavilions open onto a setting suffused with an aura of serenity, a garden path (*roji*) laid with flat stones that meander toward a stream. Before entering the house, the visitor must wash his hands, drawing the water with a bamboo ladle; he takes off his shoes and jewelry. In their day, samurais left their weapons outside. The entryway is low so that the visitor must stoop to enter as a sign of humility. A landscape print (*kakemono*) hangs on the wall and a humble bouquet of seasonal flowers decorates an alcove (*tokonoma*). A tatami of braided bamboo covers the floor. The décor (*wabi*) is spare, sober, and refined. The visitor kneels and the ceremony begins. The mistress of the house places

The
Cha
No
Yu

"To make a delicious bowl of tea
lay the charcoal so that it heats
the water.
Arrange the flowers as if they
are in the field.
Suggest coolness in summer
and warmth in winter.
Do everything ahead of time
Prepare for rain.
Make every possible
consideration for your guests."
SEN NO RIKYU

an iron kettle (*kama*) over a brazier, gently heating the water. She delicately holds the lacquer caddy (*natsume*), in which the Matcha green tea is carefully stored, and with a spatula, she puts the leaves in a ceramic bowl (*chawan*). She carefully wipes the spatula and pours a bit of hot water over the tea powder. The mixture is whipped with a bamboo whisk (*chasen*) until it turns into a "jade mousse," ready to be shared with guests. A pastry or light meal (*kaiseki*) complements the tea's slightly bitter aftertaste.

Moroccan mint tea

Unlike the tea ceremonies in China or Japan, which take place in tea houses, the sharing of tea in Morocco is much more familial and friendly.

The mint green tea ritual is very popular here. The drink is offered all day long in public squares, in hotels, in nomad tents out in the desert, and in the souks. However, the true ceremony usually takes place in the home. It symbolizes sharing and hospitality. Fatema Hal, author and director of the restaurant La Mansouria in Paris, recounts the following:

Below: Traditional glasses for serving mint tea. Moroccan reproductions of glasses made by Saint-Louis.

"In my country, people taste and offer green tea all day long. We serve Gunpowder imported from China with sprigs of mint. This offering is a sign of welcome. Tea is never served in the kitchen; this would be a serious insult. Trays are always ready in the living room, suggesting that your arrival is awaited.

"On the first tray there are teacups and one or two teapots along with a silver glass or tachilila. On a second tray, the mistress of the house places a silver service or r'biaa, a sugar bowl, a sugar loaf, a small copper hammer, and a cup with mint ready to be served as well as a smaller container for the Gunpowder. In winter, when the mint is less fragrant, a bit of fresh absinthe (schiba) is added.

"In the past, a cauldron or kanoune was placed above the charcoal to heat the water; today it has been replaced by a kettle.

"Two sheer muslin cloths, often embroidered, cover the trays. A vial of orange flower water is available to perfume the guests; several drops are often poured into the tea.

"During the ceremony, the teapot is rinsed with boiling water before it is filled with the tea and mint; the

equivalent of one glass of water is added. This mixture is quickly stirred and this first infusion is then poured away into the silver glass. The sugar loaf is broken up with the hammer and added to the teapot with very hot water. After this second infusion steeps for three to four minutes, the teapot is lifted high above the glasses to serve the tea. This gesture is based on a folkloric belief that mixing the oxygen with the tea improves digestion.

"This is how tea is served in middle-class homes. In the country, an enamel teapot is more commonly used, and they do without a separate kettle. Once the tea is prepared, the teapot is placed directly over the heat. In the towns and northern regions of the country, the tea, served in pretty colored glasses, is clearer and lighter than the tea served in the south. There it is more opaque and concentrated, stronger, and more bitter, but it is still served with an open-hearted generosity.

"As in China and Japan, the tea is served with small cakes such as crescent-shaped pastries flavored with green tea."

In Morocco, green mint tea is served in metal teapots (right). It can also be prepared in a glass teapot (above).

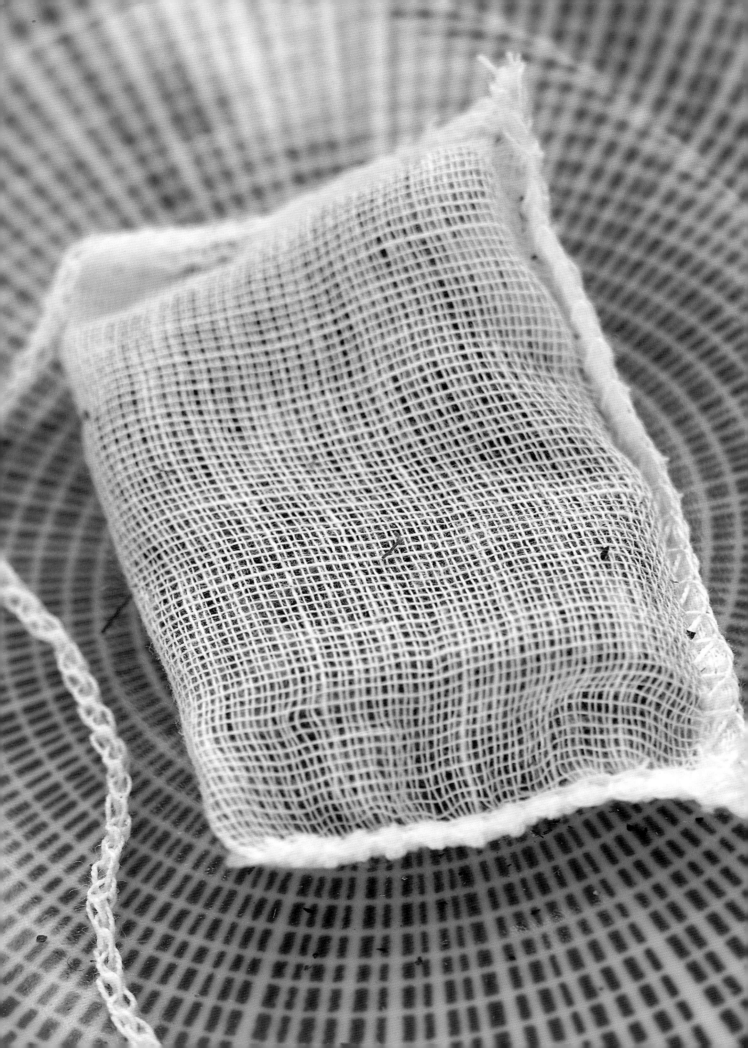

Secrets of tea preparation

Left: A beautiful handmade
pure-cotton muslin sachet,
without glue or staples:
the only packaging for
sachets that does not alter
the taste of the tea.

In addition to the choice of water and tea variety, the teapot is essential to the preparation of a high-quality liquor. In general, teapots must be used only for one type of tea as many of them become "seasoned," taking on the taste of the tea. Preference should be given to teapots that have handles molded separately from the body, which hinder the transfer of heat and reduce the risk of burns. Attention should also be paid to the spout, which must not drip during service.

Clay and cast-iron teapots

In the morning, one might use a Chinese teapot made of unglazed terra cotta, with a large clay filter that allows the leaves to unfurl freely. Clay seasons very well and takes on the taste of the tea. Among clay pots, those from the region of Yixing are esteemed for their various shapes and colors. These teapots are often unique pieces, made by hand using traditional methods.

Japanese cast-iron teapots are perfect for Lung Ching tea. These beautiful objects retain the heat and season well, without being fragile. Their capacity is limited to four to six pints. They should be well dried after rinsing.

The interiors of cast-iron teapots made in Japan are often enamel. They can be used with very pretty opaline or decorative glass teacups, which are sometimes lightly colored with the same enamel as the teapot.

Below: A Chinese bamboo
strainer used to filter
loose tea.

Porcelain and earthenware teapots

Porcelain teapots are ideal for Sunday tea: a Darjeeling, for example, can be enjoyed with the family or among friends, and is the perfect elixir for a delightful afternoon. A factory in Saint Petersburg has reissued delicate blue cobalt sets of very fine quality.

It is best to choose a porcelain teapot with a flanged lid that can hold the top firmly in place while pouring. As these teapots rarely come with an integrated filter, a "sock," a textile or paper filter is required. If none is available, pure-cotton muslin tea sachets may be used; they should be hand sewn and free of any staples or starch.

English earthenware teapots can be whimsical or classic. Since the 1980s, they have been made in many different shapes and colors to meet a wide range of tastes and appeal to many collectors. They are appropriate for the same types of tea as porcelain pots.

Glass and silver teapots

Glass teapots from Italy or Germany are well suited to flavored teas. They can be washed, and since they do not retain the flavor of the tea, they can be used for different varieties. They often come with a large built-in glass filter that allows the leaves to swirl freely.

Three types of teapots: a German glass teapot with filter, ideal for flavored teas (above); a Japanese cast-iron teapot with a built-in metal filter that helps control the infusion time (right); an enamel English teapot designed as a cup, eccentric reproduction of aviator model (below).

Garden of Mogador, a Moroccan green mint flavored tea, or Tea On the Veranda, flavored with cherry and rose, are a pure pleasure when served in these teapots.

Silver or silver-plate teapots from Morocco, without filters, are perfect for fresh mint tea, with the leaves simply placed in the bottom of the pot. Small rings on the handle act as insulation.

With this wide selection of choices, tea aficionados often find them-selves becoming collectors of teapots.

Bamboo whisks for preparing powdered teas such as Matcha, used in the Japanese tea ceremony (above right). It is better to use a paper filter (above left) than a wire mesh ball, which alters the taste of the tea and prevents the leaves from developing fully (below).

Choosing a tea

There are many excellent shops that offer a wide range of very high qual-ity tea. The sellers know their product and are reliable guides, inviting the client to smell, examine, touch, taste and even listen to the noise made by the broken leaves of the various teas on offer. By "crunching" several tea leaves, the buyer can get a precise idea of how the infusion will taste.

Many shops also offer tastings to their clients, thereby giving the tea lover the ability to experiment with new flavors. Remember to tell the merchant what time you like to drink your tea, as this information is essential to choosing a tea best suited to you.

The choice of tea, the
temperature of the water and
a neutral pH level, as well as the
time of infusion, are key elements
for a successful cup of tea
(above).

The secrets of infusion

As a general rule of thumb, the appropriate measurement for tea is one teaspoon per cup plus one for the pot. In order to prevent spoiling the taste of the tea, it is best to use water with a neutral pH level or filtered water, making sure to adjust the temperature to the variety of tea chosen.

When the water begins to boil in a kettle, it has reached a temperature of between 194 and 203°F. This is the ideal temperature for Orange Pekoe black teas or Flowery Orange Pekoes, which should be infused for three to five minutes. For Broken Orange Pekoes, the infusion time should be limited to three minutes.

With green tea, the maximum water temperature is 158°F with one to five minutes for infusion. The Japanese Gyokuro tea is best prepared at 140°F, and the infusion time should not exceed one minute.

White teas release their flavor when the water temperature is 140°F and the tea has been infused for seven to 20 minutes.

Following double page: Different
green tea infusions: Gunpowder,
Gyokuro and Lung Ching.

Flavored teas need not infuse for more than three to four minutes in water of 158–185°F. Boiling water destroys the flavor.

91

These directions may appear a bit complicated, but rest assured. With a little experience, you will find a tea that perfectly suits your taste.

Storing tea

To store tea properly, it should be placed in a sealed metal container. Protected from air and light, it can be stored for several months, or even years, without losing its freshness.

Flavored green teas

In France and in some other European countries, tea drinkers are showing a stronger preference for green teas, particularly toward flavored ones such as Earl Grey from Cherche-Midi, a blend of green and blue-green tea with a touch of natural orange essence, or Tea On the Veranda, a Sencha green tea with the aroma of cherries and rose petals that is delicious hot or cold.

Flavored teas have also inspired chefs, who are using their talents to incorporate them into their recipes. Take Massimo Mori at Emporio Armani for example, who spices his risotto with Mao Jian green tea leaves from China, or Emmanuel Laporte from Les Feuilles Libres in Neuilly, who uses green tea to flavor veal chops or enhance the taste of chocolate bonbons.

While the interest in flavored green teas is fairly recent in Europe, it is an ancient tradition in China, where certain teas have been flavored with jasmine, lotus or chrysanthemums for centuries.

Citrus fruits are used in several flavored green teas: Toudra green tea with peels of orange (above), grapefruit (right) and lemon (below).

94

陳

陳百

郎 海 山

隆 興 股

錦 發

森

、

曾

莫　　秋 　　陳 　　
駐 斯 　　復 　　　
　榴 　　受 　
　　　　九

From the Cup to the Plate

How can tea be transformed into a cooking ingredient without distorting or altering its very nature? Can it be removed from the realm of beverages, while respecting and even enhancing its distinctive characteristics? How should tea be combined with other ingredients?

In preparing a recipe, tea should be treated as a unique ingredient. The art of incorporating tea into a recipe is not a matter of skilful camouflage; instead, it is a happy marriage, where each partner maintains its integrity while contributing to the ultimate success of the union.

Tea leaves work wonders with cakes and fillings. Teas flavored with fruit or spices blend harmoniously into sorbets or frozen desserts. Infused in milk, cream or fruit juice, tea lends a breath of inspiration to creams, flans, and sauces.

Michèle Carles

Terrine of chicken and shrimp with Sencha Toundra green tea

Serves 6 to 8

1 1/8 lbs. chicken filets

1 1/4 lbs. shrimp

1 oz. Sencha Toundra green tea

12 fl. oz. ultra pasteurized cream

2 eggs

2 teaspoons salt

3 pinches of pepper

1 *bouquet garni*

a few Sencha Toundra

green tea leaves

1 or 2 lemons

Paul Conan,

for Jérôme Nagat,

Aux Mille Délices

Bring the cream and tea to a boil and infuse 10 minutes. Season the chicken filets with salt and pepper, then blend.

Add the tea-infused cream (reserving the tea leaves) and the eggs. Set the cream and chicken mixture aside and keep chilled.

Fill a stockpot with water. Add the *bouquet garni* and bring to a boil. Immerse the shrimp in the boiling water for 5 minutes. Drain the shrimp, allow them to cool, and remove the shells.

Spread half the chicken and cream mixture in a terrine. Arrange the shrimp on top and pour over the remaining chicken and cream mixture. Bake in a hot water bath for 1 hour. Chill and unmold.

Garnish decoratively with a few green tea leaves and some lemon wedges. Serve well chilled accompanied by a salad dressed with lemon vinaigrette.

Breast of guinea hen flavored with Bancha Hojicha tea, with sugar snap peas, green asparagus, and chives

Serves 4

1 guinea hen

3/4 oz. roasted Bancha Hojicha green tea

1 lb. sugar snap peas

16 green asparagus

2 chive stalks

8.5 fl. oz. chicken broth

3 1/2 tbsp. butter

2 teaspoons *fleur de sel*

freshly ground pepper

Philippe Renard,

Hôtel Lutétia

Clean the sugar snap peas and the asparagus. Blanch them in 5,5 quarts of boiling salted water, then plunge in ice water.
Cut the guinea hen into 8 pieces. Season them and brown in the butter. Mince and add the chives.
Moisten with the chicken broth, and cook covered over low heat for 25 to 30 minutes.
Add the sugar snap peas, the asparagus tips, and the asparagus stalks cut into large slices. At the end of the cooking time, add the tea leaves and cook 5 minutes more. Adjust the seasoning and bind the sauce with a piece of cold butter. Strain the sauce through a sieve.
Arrange the pieces of guinea hen and vegetables in shallow bowls. Serve very hot.

Risotto "to the Ranee's taste"
with Mao Jian green tea

For each serving

3/8 cup Arborio rice

2 frog legs

2 teaspoons China Mao Jian
green tea

vegetable bouillon

2 teaspoons Parmesan cheese

2 teaspoons sugar

1 tablespoon unsalted butter

Italian parsley

salt and freshly ground pepper

extra virgin olive oil

Massimo Mori,

Emporio Armani

Steep half the tea in 12 fl. oz. water. Add the sugar and reduce the infusion until the liquid becomes caramelized.

Cook the rice in the vegetable bouillon (prepared in advance using a celery stalk, a carrot, and two onions). The rice should be cooked over medium heat for about 20 minutes until *al dente*.

As soon as the rice is ready, remove it from the heat and add the butter, the Parmesan cheese (this process is called *mantecare*) and the rest of the tea.

In a non-stick pan, brown the frogs legs in olive oil. Add the parsley and season with salt and pepper.

Mound the risotto into a "Chinese hat" style white porcelain bowl. Drizzle a ribbon of the caramelized tea infusion over the rice and add the frog legs.

Roasted breast of Bresse Guinea Hen
"with authentic smoked *tea jus*"

Serves 4

1 3/4 lbs. breast of guinea hen

a pinch of "Great Wall" tea leaves

from Contes de thé

2 lbs. celeriac

1 bunch of carrots with their greens

3.5 oz bulgur wheat

1 quart chicken bouillon

salt and freshly ground pepper

•For the chicken juice:

1 carrot

1 onion

1 chicken bouillon cube

Michel Lentz,

Hôtel Royal Parc Évian

(a fusion cuisine recipe)

Soak the tea leaves in hot water. Debone breasts and slide a tea leaf under the skin of each breast.

Season the breasts with salt and pepper. Arrange them skin side down in an oiled skillet. Add a small piece of butter to help them to brown. Cook until the skin is crisp.

Peel and cube the celeriac. Peel the carrots and set aside the greens. Wash the vegetables, and cook them in mineral water. Add them to the guinea hen and cook about 5 minutes more, until the vegetables are nicely browned.

Cook the bulgur in the chicken bouillon until it is very soft. Add the tea leaves at the end of the cooking time.

Prepare the chicken juice. Put the bouillon cube, carrots and onions into 1 quart of boiling water. Remove 1 pint of the bouillon and bring it to a boil. Add the tea, and allow it to steep. Reduce the pan juices and adjust the seasonings.

Mound the bulgur in the center of the plate. Arrange the guinea hen pieces and vegetables on top. Brown the green tea leaves very lightly in a pan for 2 or 3 minutes, being careful not to allow them to take on too much color. Sprinkle them over the dish and garnish with a ribbon of the reduced pan juices.

Veal chops with green tea

Serves 4

4 veal chops

3 teaspoons Sencha green tea

2 cups small white onions

4 carrots

2 heads of garlic, unpeeled

2 large pieces of salted butter

2 tablespoons powdered sugar

2 tablespoons olive oil

salt and pepper

Emmanuel Laporte,

Les Feuilles Libres

Peel the onions and carrots. Cut the carrots into slices

In a cast-iron pan, sauté the heads of garlic, the onions, and the carrot slices in the salted butter. Add the sugar and let the mixture brown over low heat for 15 minutes.

Brush the veal chops with the olive oil. Season them with salt and pepper and sauté them for 5 minutes in a skillet.

Steep the green tea for 3 minutes in 2 cups simmering water. Strain.

Arrange the veal chops over the vegetables. Add the infused tea and cook for 20 minutes over low heat.

Serve the veal chops from the pan.

102

Lamb chops with a crust of Matcha tea and sweet potato purée

Serves 4

2 racks of lamb, each with 6 chops

2 teaspoons. powdered Matcha tea

1 lb. sweet potatoes

3 1/2 tablespoons dry bread crumbs

1 pint milk

1 1/2 tablespoons coconut milk

3 1/2 tablespoons softened butter

sunflower oil

salt and pepper

**Walter Deshayes,
Bernardaud**

Sweet potato purée. ▸ Peel the sweet potatoes and cut them into large pieces. Cook them in a pot with the milk, the coconut milk, and a pinch of salt. When they are tender, drain them in a colander and purée them in a food processor with a slice of butter. Adjust the seasoning. If the purée is too liquid, drain it again through a clean towel. Set aside and refrigerate.

Matcha tea butter. ▸ Blend the softened butter with the tea. Add the bread crumbs, season to taste, and set aside to cool.

Lamb chops. ▸ Brush the racks of lamb with sunflower oil, season with salt and pepper, and roast them in the oven for 10 to 12 minutes. Remove the racks of lamb from the oven, cut them into chops and lay them on a baking pan. Put a large piece of Matcha tea butter on each chop and slide them under the broiler for just a few seconds; do not allow the butter to brown.

To serve. ▸ reheat the sweet potato purée. Melt a little of the Matcha tea butter. On each plate, decoratively arrange 3 chops and 3 mounds of sweet potato purée. Surround the chops and purée with a ribbon of melted Matcha tea butter.

Chazuké or Japanese Leftovers

For each serving

1/2 cup leftover rice

1 teaspoon Sencha green tea

a few pieces of dried or grilled fish

When you have a little rice left over from last night's dinner, you can use it to make *chazuké*, a very popular Japanese recipe.

Prepare the Sencha green tea and pour the infusion over the cold rice. Add the dried or grilled fish and enjoy.

Thinly sliced shrimp marinated in green tea

Serves 6 to 8

5 1/2 lb. shrimp

1 teaspoon Lung Ching green tea

2 limes

1 orange

2 cups olive oil

1/2 cup piquillo peppers

2 teaspoons *fleur de sel*

1 teaspoon freshly ground pepper

Michel Hache,

Hôtel Ambassador

Squeeze the limes and orange and infuse the Lung Ching green tea in their juice. Meanwhile, peel and devein the shrimp. Cut the shrimp into fine slices, drizzle them with olive oil and season to taste. Set aside.

When ready to serve, arrange the shrimp on clear glass serving plates with the help of a circular mold or small bowl. Sprinkle with the minced piquillo pepper and cover with the tea infusion.

Filets of sole in an infusion of Gyokuro green tea, with fava beans and baby carrots and tomato confit

Serves 4

4 filets of sole, weighing 2/3 lb. each

1 1/2 tablespoons Gyokuro tea

4 1/2 lbs. fava beans

8 baby carrots

4 tomatoes

4 small onions

3 1/2 tablespoons butter

2 teaspoons *fleur de sel*

1.7 fl. oz. virgin olive oil

1 teaspoon granulated sugar

3 1/2 tablespoons chicken stock

Espelette pepper

Philippe Renard,

Hôtel Lutétia

Peel the tomatoes. (You may put them in boiling water for 30 seconds to simplify this procedure.) Cut them in half and remove the seeds and membranes. Season with olive oil, sugar, and salt and slowly bake them in a preheated 175 °F oven for 6 hours.

Shell the fava beans, blanch them and remove their skins. Peel the carrots and the onions and blanch them in 1 quart of boiling salted water.

Season with salt and pepper and add the Espelette pepper to taste. Sauté the filets of sole in butter.

Cook the vegetables in the chicken stock; they must remain crisp. Add the tea leaves at the end of the cooking time and let them steep for 5 minutes. Whisk the bouillon with the cool butter. Strain the sauce through a sieve, then cover the filets with it. Adjust the seasoning and serve the fish together with the vegetables in shallow bowls.

Tajine of Williams pears with green tea and dried fruit and nuts

Serves 4

4 William pears

1 1/2 tbsp. Sencha O.P. green tea

1 oz. honey

2 tsp. raisins

2 tsp. whole almonds

2 tsp. dried apricots

2 tsp. pistachios

2 tsp. pine nuts

1/2 cup orange juice

1 cinnamon stick

1 star anise

6 mint leaves

Walter Deshayes,
Bernardaud

Peel and quarter the pears and remove the cores and seeds. Caramelize the honey. Add the pears, the spices, and the dried fruits and combine well. Place the green tea in a "sock" and add to the mixture, then deglaze with the orange juice.

Cook, covered, for 15 minutes, watching carefully so that the juice does not reduce too much. If necessary, add a bit of orange juice (or substitute a little water). When the cooking is complete, the juice should be bright in color with a lightly syrupy consistency.

Remove the tea "sock." Add the mint leaves, torn gently with your fingers, and serve in covered bowls, or, preferably, in small tajines.

Gratin of white peaches with Japanese green tea and kaffir lime zest

Serves 6

3 1/4 lbs. white peaches

2 teaspoons Japanese
gyokura green tea

2 teaspoons kaffir lime zest
(if unavailable, you may
substitute regular lime)

3/4 cup sugar

juice of 1 lemon

1 1/4 cup whole milk

1 lemon leaf

2 1/2 tablespoons cornstarch

1 egg yolk

5 tablespoons. mixed flower honey

1 cup *crème fleurette*

brown sugar

a few pine nuts

a few cubes of crystallized ginger

6 tablespoons confectioners sugar

Patrick Loustalot-Barbe,
L'Artisan de Saveurs

Prepare the peaches the day before. ▶ Peel the peaches. (To simplify this procedure, you may immerse the peaches for 30 seconds in boiling water, then plunge them in ice water.)

Poach the peaches 30 to 40 minutes in a pot containing 1 quart of water, the lemon juice and the sugar, taking care not to allow the liquid to come to a full boil. Cool and set the peaches aside in their cooking juice. Poaching the peaches the day before makes them easier to pit and cut.

Prepare the whipped cream the day before. ▶ Beat the *crème fleurette* gently, without letting it get too stiff.

Prepare the pastry cream the day before. ▶ In a bowl, combine the honey, the cornstarch and the egg yolk. Combine the lemon leaf, the kaffir lime zest, the tea and the milk. Bring the mixture to a simmer. Remove from the heat and allow to infuse 1 minute. Strain the milk mixture through a sieve into the honey mixture. Whisk together lightly and return the combined mixture to the heat, stirring constantly at a boil for 1 minute. Remove from the heat, and, while still warm, gradually fold in the whipped cream. Place the pastry cream in the refrigerator overnight so that the flavors will blend.

Presentation and final preparation. ▶ Remove the pits from the peaches and slice. Arrange the slices on plates. Cover the fruit with the pastry cream and sprinkle with a pinch of brown sugar. Brown the dessert in the oven and serve warm, sprinkled with lightly toasted pine nuts, cubes of crystallized ginger, and a dusting of confectioners' sugar.

Serve the dessert with iced green tea, sweetened with the cooking juice from the peaches.

Chilled rhubarb soup with Matcha tea and Mara wild strawberries

Serves 6

1 lb. Mara wild strawberries

2 lbs. rhubarb

2 teaspoons Matcha tea

1 cup sugar

juice of 1 lemon

1 cup plain yogurt

1/2 cup cream

1 3/4 cup sugar

6 almond *tuile* cookies

Patrick Loustalot-Barbe,
l'Artisan de saveurs

The day before serving the dish, wash, dry and hull the strawberries. Peel the rhubarb and cut it into 1/2 inch slices. Bring 1 quart of water to a boil with the sugar and the lemon juice. Immerse the rhubarb in the boiling water and poach about 15 minutes; do not allow the mixture to come to a full boil. Drain the rhubarb and set aside 3/4 cup of the cooking liquid. Place the rhubarb in a large bowl and chill in a larger container of ice cubes.

In a mixing bowl, combine half the rhubarb, the yogurt, the reserved cooking liquid and the tea. Bring the cream and sugar to a boil. Combine the hot cream mixture with the rhubarb mixture and blend in a food processor. Set aside to cool.

Pour the rhubarb and Matcha green tea soup into 6 small dishes. Arrange the remaining rhubarb on top and garnish with the wild strawberries cut into quarters or halves. Serve with almond *tuiles*.

"Mogador Garden" brioche

Serves 8 to 10

3 1/4 cups flour

4 eggs

5 tablespoons sugar

2 teaspoons salt

1 capful crème de menthe

2 tablespoons powdered "Mogador Garden" tea (ground in a food processor)

1 3/4 tablespoons yeast

5 tablespoons unsalted butter

Alexis Riou,
for Jérôme Nagat,
Aux Mille Délices

Place the flour, eggs, 1,5 fl. oz. of water, sugar, salt, crème de menthe, yeast, and tea in a food processor. Blend 12 minutes at slow speed. Add the butter and process until the dough comes together.

Remove the dough from the food processor and form it into a ball. Sprinkle the dough with flour and cover with a towel. Let it rest 1 hour. Knead the dough again and shape it into one large or several smaller balls. Set aside for an additional 1 1/2 hours.

Preheat the oven to 410°F. Bake the brioche 25 minutes, just until lightly browned. Cool before serving.

Strawberries with "Mogador Garden" confit

Serves 6

2 lbs. strawberries

1/2 jar "Mogador Garden" tea confit

from Contes de thé

a few mint leaves

•For the iced tea:

2 teaspoons "Mogador Garden" tea

from Contes de thé

Philippe et Sylvie Charpentier,

Les Jardins d'Hélény

Wash and hull the strawberries.

Dilute the tea confit with 1 cup of water. Blend thoroughly and pour the syrup over the strawberries. Refrigerate the fruit mixture.

When you are ready to serve, garnish decoratively with a few mint leaves.

Serve with an infusion of iced tea prepared the day before. Contrary to what you might assume, it is better to let the tea infuse overnight in cold water in the refrigerator and strain it the next morning. The infusion will be unclouded and will have more flavor.

Green tea macaroons

Makes 15 macaroons

1/2 cup ground almonds

1 cup confectioners' sugar

2 teaspoons green tea

3 egg whites

4 teaspoons granulated sugar

•For the butter cream:

1 fl. oz. crème anglaise

3 1/2 tablespoons butter

1 teaspoon green tea

Nicolas Boussin, sur l'initiative

de Christelle Vandaele,

la Grande Épicerie

Combine the ground almonds, the confectioners' sugar and the green tea. Beat the egg whites, gradually adding the granulated sugar; then add the almond, sugar, and tea mixture.

Knead until the dough is very smooth. Spread greaseproof paper on a baking tray and form the dough into small cookies. Bake at 320°F for 12 minutes with the oven door partly open.

Meanwhile, prepare the filling by combining the butter with the tea. Add the crème anglaise gradually, whisking to blend. Set aside.

When the macaroons are baked, take the baking tray from the oven. Remove the greaseproof paper, moisten the bottom and replace it on the baking tray. Let cool several minutes, then remove the cookies. To serve, sandwich together 2 cookies with a spoonful of butter cream.

113

Chocolate tart with "Mogador Garden" green tea

Serves 6 to 8

•For the pastry:

2 1/2 cups flour

1 cup butter

pinch of salt

1 cup confectioners' sugar

2 eggs

1/4 cup ground almonds

3 tablespoons cocoa powder

•For the tea filling:

2 1/2 tablespoons "Mogador Garden" green tea

8.5 fl. oz. ultra pasteurized cream

1 cup dark chocolate squares

8.5 fl. oz. glucose syrup

Stéphane Henriot,

for Jérôme Nagat,

Aux Mille Délices

Put the flour on a working surface and make a well in the middle. Drop the sugar, salt, butter cut up into small pieces, eggs, ground almonds, and cocoa powder into the well. Combine the ingredients, working the dough lightly with your fingertips. As soon as it no longer sticks to your fingers, form it into a ball.

Seal the dough in a plastic food storage bag and refrigerate for 1 hour.

Remove the dough from the refrigerator and press it into a buttered tart pan. Set aside.

Preheat the oven to 350 °F. Bake the pastry shell about 10 minutes, weighting it down with dried beans. Allow to cool, then refrigerate.

Bring the cream and the tea to a boil and infuse 10 minutes. Strain through a sieve, then add the glucose syrup, and chocolate. Return to low heat and pour the mixture into the pastry shell.

Keep the tart in the refrigerator until ready to serve. Garnish decoratively with a dusting of confectioners' sugar and mint leaves.

Vanilla ice cream with Saint-Sylvester tea confit

For a jar of confit

2 cups Saint-Sylvester tea

10 cups sugar

2 tablespoons lemon juice

For each serving:

2 scoops of vanilla ice cream

2-3 tablespoons green tea confit

ground cinnamon

1 small cinnamon stick

Henri Burgos,

Les Délices du Roy

Tea confit. ▸ Soak the Saint-Sylvester tea in 6 cups boiling water for about 15 minutes. Reheat the infusion, and as soon as it starts to boil, add the sugar. As soon as it returns to a boil, stir constantly for 4 minutes, then add the lemon juice. Pour the mixture into sterilized jars. Return them to heat for a few minutes more to ensure proper preservation.

To serve. ▸ Place 2 scoops of ice cream in each dessert bowl. Add 2 or 3 spoonfuls of the Saint-Sylvester tea confit, and sprinkle with ground cinnamon. Garnish with a cinnamon stick and serve immediately.

Bittersweet chocolate candies
with green tea caramel

Makes about 50 chocolate candies

1 3/4 cups dark sweeet chocolate

3 1/2 tablespoons milk chocolate

1 tablespoon China green tea

1 3/4 tablespoons *crème fleurette*

1/2 cup granulated sugar

1 teaspoon lemon juice

Robert Linxe,
La Maison du Chocolat

Chop the dark and milk chocolates finely and place them in a large bowl.

Put the sugar in a pot with a tablespoon of water. Cook over low heat until lightly caramelized.

In another pot, bring the cream to a boil.

Add the tea to the hot cream and allow it to infuse for 4 or 5 minutes. Strain the cream mixture over the chocolate.

Wait 20 seconds, then stir the mixture gently with a whisk until the ingredients are just combined. Add the caramel and whisk together. Add the lemon juice and whisk together 4 minutes more, just until the mixture is smooth.

Spread the mixture 1/2 inch thick on heavy plastic wrap. Allow it to cool and become firm before cutting into small rectangles. You may also pour the mixture into a small pastry bag and form small balls, allowing them to become firm. Serve the chocolates with dessert.

Two-tone madeleines
with two teas

Makes 24 madeleines

•For the Matcha tea dough:

3/4 cup flour

7 tablespoons butter

1/2 cup granulated sugar

2 eggs

1 teaspoon Matcha tea

1 teaspoon baking powder

•For the Lung Ching dough:

3/4 cup flour

7 tablespoons butter

1/2 cup granulated sugar

2 eggs

1 teaspoon Lung Ching green tea

1 teaspoon baking powder

Michèle Carles,

food writer

Preheat the oven to 400 °F.

Matcha tea dough. ▶ Melt the butter over low heat in a small pot, then let it cool. Combine the flour, baking powder and tea in a bowl.
Break the eggs into another bowl and whisk them with the sugar until they are lemon colored. Add the flour mixture. Mix in the butter and blend together.

Lung Ching dough. ▶ Melt the butter over low heat in a small pot, then let it cool.
Crush the tea between your fingertips.
Combine the flour, baking powder and tea in a bowl.
Break the eggs into another bowl and whisk them with the sugar until they are lemon colored. Add the flour mixture. Mix in the butter and blend together.

Madeleines. ▶ Butter a madeleine tin and drop a teaspoon of each dough into the mold. Bake 5 minutes before lowering the temperature to 350 °F. Bake an additional 10 minutes. When the madeleines are ready, take them out of the oven, remove them from the tin and allow to cool.

Gazelle horn cookies with Khaab-el-Ghozal green tea

Makes 25 gazelle horn cookies

•For the almond paste:

2 1/2 cups shelled almonds

2 cups powdered sugar

2 tablespoons infused green
Gunpowder tea

1 tablespoon melted butter

•For the dough:

2 cups flour

2 teaspoon infused green
Gunpowder tea

1 tablespoon melted butter

**Fatema Hal,
le Mansouria**

Almond paste. ▸ Boil water and infuse the tea. Strain the tea and set aside, reserving the leaves. Brown the leaves in a small amount of butter. Combine the almonds and the sugar and process into a paste in a food mill. Knead the almond paste, adding the infused tea, the melted butter and the browned tea leaves. Roll the paste into balls the size of a walnut, and form them into cigar-shaped cylinders.

Dough. ▸ Preheat the oven to 480 °F. Combine all the ingredients; the dough will be stiff. Roll out the dough as thinly as possible. On one half of the dough, place the almond paste cigars at regularly spaced intervals and fold the remaining half of the dough over them. Cut around each cylinder with a roller, seal the edges, and shape into crescents. Poke several holes in each crescent with a thin knitting needle. Brush with egg white and bake in the oven for about 10 minutes. The gazelle horns should be very lightly browned.

Red currant and Morello cherry preserves with green tea

Makes ten jars

3 1/4 lb. very ripe Morello cherries

3 1/4 lb. red currants

2 tablespoons China Zhejiang

Gunpowder green tea

juice of 1 pesticide-free lemon

6 1/2 lb. refined cane sugar

1/2 teaspoon agar

or 2 1/2 tablespoon apple pectin

Henri Burgos,

Les Délices du Roy

Soak the tea in 2 cups water at 195°F for at least 15 or 20 minutes.

Rinse and clean the currants. Place them in a cooking pot with the infused tea and cook over high heat 8 to 10 minutes until the fruits burst. Pass through the finest strainer of a food mill to extract a smooth purée.

Clean and pit the cherries and place them in a preserve pot. Add the currant purée. Bring the fruit mixture to a boil and immediately add 6 lb. of sugar cup by cup. Mix the agar or apple pectin with the remaining sugar. Add this sugar and the lemon juice to the preserves after 20 minutes of cooking at a simmer.

Fill glass jars, and return them to the heat for a few minutes to sterilize the tops. Store the jars away from light and humidity.

Mogador tea *gelée* with lemon sorbet

For each cup of *gelée*

3 tablespoons Mogador tea

10 cups sugar

2 teaspoons lemon juice

For each serving:

2 scoops of lemon sorbet

2 to 3 teaspoons tea *gelée*

a few fresh mint leaves

a few rose petals

Henri Burgos,

les Délices du Roy

Tea gelée. ▸ Soak the tea in 6 cups of boiling water for about 15 minutes. Bring to a boil. When the first bubbles appear, add the sugar. As soon as the liquid returns to a boil, stir constantly for 4 minutes; then add the lemon juice. Pour the mixture into sterilized jars. Return them to the heat for a few minutes to ensure proper preservation

To serve. ▸ Place 2 scoops of lemon sorbet in dessert bowls. Add 2 or 3 spoonfuls of the Mogador tea *gelée*, and garnish with mint leaves and rose petals. Serve immediately.

Chilled parfaits with Genmaicha tea and wild strawberries

Serves 6

1 1/2 lbs. wild strawberries

•For the parfait:

3/4 cup cream

3/4 cup milk

1 1/2 tablespoon Genmaicha tea

3 egg yolks

1/4 cup granulated sugar

1 cup whipped cream

1/4 cup puffed rice

•For the almond milk:

1/2 cup whole milk

3 1/2 tablespoons almond paste

•For the Genmaicha whipped cream:

1 1/4 cup cream

2 teaspoons Genmaicha tea

2 teaspoons confectioners' sugar

•For the Balinese pepper crunch:

3 1/2 tablespoons sliced almonds

1/2 cup granulated sugar

a pinch of ground Balinese pepper

•For the crisp tea wafers:

1 1/4 cup confectioners' sugar

5 tablespoons flour

1/4 cup orange juice

4 tablespoons melted butter

a few sprigs of tea

Thierry Bridron, pastry chef,

Hôtel Lutétia

Parfait. ▸ Bring the cream and milk to a boil. Add the tea and allow it to infuse 5 minutes. Strain through a sieve. In a pot, whisk the egg yolks and the granulated sugar with until the yolks are lemon colored. Pour in the cream and milk mixture and finish cooking as you would a *crème anglaise*. Remove from the heat and whisk until completely cooled. Fold in the whipped cream and then the puffed rice. Spoon into molds 8 cm in diameter and place them in the freezer.

Almond milk. ▸ Bring the milk to a boil and pour it over the almond paste. Blend thoroughly together and set aside in a cool place.

Genmaicha whipped cream. ▸ Bring 1/3 of the cream to a boil with the tea. Allow to infuse 5 minutes, then strain through a sieve. Add the remaining chilled cream and the confectioners' sugar. Refrigerate for 2 hours. Whip the cream before serving.

Balinese pepper crunch. ▸ Brown the sliced almonds in the oven at 320 °F. Bring 1/4 cup water to a boil with the granulated sugar. Add the almonds and the pepper and combine. Spread on a baking pan and dry in the oven at 100 °C until the sugar is crystallized.

Crisp tea wafers. ▸ Combine the sugar, flour, orange juice and melted butter. Form the mixture into 3-inch rounds and arrange them on parchment paper. Sprinkle with a few tea leaves and bake at 212 °F until lightly browned.

Service and presentation. ▸ Unmold a parfait onto each plate. Cover with a tea wafer and top with wild strawberries. Serve with a dollop of Genmaicha whipped cream, some pepper crunch and a splash of almond milk.

Chocolate *"bonbons"* with green tea and passion fruit seeds

Serves 4

7 oz. bittersweet dark chocolate

4 teaspoons Sencha green tea

2 passion fruit

4 sheets phyllo pastry

1/2 cup cream (30% milkfat content)

1 teaspoon butter

Emmanuel Laporte,

Les Feuilles Libres

Bring the cream to a boil. Remove from the heat and add the tea. Allow to infuse 3 minutes and strain. Add the chocolate and allow it to melt without stirring. When the chocolate is melted, whisk the mixture just until it is well blended. Cover the bottom of a mold with greaseproof paper. Pour the mixture into the mold and store overnight in the refrigerator.

Cut the chocolate mixture into small rectangles. Preheat the oven to 410 °F. Lay out 2 leaves of phyllo pastry and brush them with butter. Arrange the chocolate rectangles on top of the phyllo, spacing them evenly. Brush the remaining phyllo sheets with butter and lay them over the chocolate rectangles. Cut the pastry into rectangles around the chocolate. Pinch the edges of each pastry rectangle into the shape of a bonbon. Bake 5 minutes.

Cut open the passion fruit and remove the seeds with a spoon. Arrange them on plates and serve them with the warm bonbons.

Pomelos with green tea *gelée*

Serves 4

6 pomelos

1 teaspoon Lung Ching green tea

3 leaves of gelatin

2 cups orange juice

1/2 cup acacia honey

1 stalk and 4 anise stars

Michel Lentz,

hôtel Royal Parc Évian

Peel and quarter the pomelos, taking care to retain the juice.

Soak the gelatin leaves in cold water. Strain the orange juice. Put the strained orange juice and the honey in a pot and cook over low heat.

Reduce the juice mixture to a syrup. In the pomelo juice, steep the green tea for 2 minutes and the anise for 5 minutes. Stir in the gelatin leaves. Chill over a bed of crushed ice.

Arrange the pomelo quarters in a circle in serving bowls, then pour over the pomelo juice halfway up the sides of the bowls. Allow it to gel. Drizzle a spoonful of orange syrup over each serving and decorate with an anise star. Serve well chilled.

Peaches with green tea *gelée*

Serves 4

2 white peaches

1 cup raspberries

or wild strawberries

2 teaspoons "Tea On the Veranda"

green tea

1/4 cup granulated sugar

4 leaves of gelatin

1 lime

a few leaves of lemon verbena

fresh lemon grass and mint

Michèle Carles,

journaliste culinaire

Soften the leaves of gelatin in cold water.

Bring 1 1/4 cup water to a boil. Add the sugar and let it dissolve. Remove from the heat. Add the tea and allow it to infuse for 4 to 5 minutes. Strain over a pot and bring the infusion to a boil. Drain the gelatin leaves and add them to the infusion. When they have dissolved, remove the pot from the heat and allow the contents to cool.

Cut the peaches into 1/2 inch slices. Place them in a large bowl and add the berries.

Finely grate the lime zest and add it to half of the tea *gelée*. Carefully turn the berries in the *gelée* so that they are thoroughly coated. Set aside and keep cool.

Spread the remaining gelée in a 1/2 inch layer on a plate. Allow it to cool, then place in the refrigerator until firm.

Unmold the *gelée*. Cut it into little cubes and scatter them over the fruits. Add the verbena leaves, the mint and the slivered lemon grass and return the dessert to the refrigerator until ready to serve.

Cocktails on the veranda

Makes 4 cocktails

1 tablespoon "Tea On the Veranda"
green tea

Gosset "*excellence brut*"
champagne

A few rose petals

**Michèle Carles,
food writer**

Bring 1 1/4 cup water to a boil and immediately remove from the heat. Add the tea. Cover and infuse for 4 minutes. Strain.

Allow the infusion to cool, then place in the refrigerator. When it is well chilled and you are ready to serve the cocktails, divide the infusion among 4 champagne flutes. Pour the champagne and serve immediately.

This tea has a China Sencha green tea base, flavored with cherry and rose petals. You may garnish the cocktails with a few rose petals from the tea.

A recipe for iced tea

Makes 1 quart

1 quart mineral water
with a neutral pH

7 or 8 teaspoons Queen of Sheba
or Black Forest flavored tea

zest from citrus fruit

Christine Dattner

Put the mineral water into a pitcher and add the tea. Do not stir; the tea leaves will sink to the bottom by themselves.

Allow the tea to infuse overnight at room temperature.

In the morning, strain and refrigerate for at least 2 hours.

Add the citrus zest just before serving.

This method produces a clear, perfectly infused beverage.

The Benefits of Green Tea

Green tea promotes good health

A traditional Chinese Yixing clay teapot. Green tea has been used in Chinese medicine for centuries.

In 2002, the world's oldest human being was a Japanese woman whose diet consisted of little more than raw fish, a bit of sake, and green tea! Green tea does more than quench thirst; its health and beauty benefits are widely recognized, and research centers all over the world are studying its many positive effects.

A valued remedy in Chinese medicine

Mrs. Ke Wan, a Chinese physician and founder of "Temps du Corps" in Paris, is a devoted green tea drinker. She explains:

"People in China are very dedicated to maintaining good health and have always drunk green tea throughout the day. They know which medicinal plant to use for what ailment and select varieties of tea depending on the problem they wish to treat. Tea removes impurities and helps clear out and strengthen the system. It is rich in vitamins and minerals. Tea boosts the immune system, improves blood circulation, sharpens vision, dispels yang (negative energy), and relieves fatigue and stress, which are both sources of hypertension. The beverage promotes yin (positive energy) and prevents certain cardiovascular problems. Green tea fights free radicals, which are a factor in the aging process. Tea helps to nourish and hydrate the skin. People in China do not drink green tea with meals, because it is believed to start a fire in the digestive system".

The list of green tea's many virtues, compiled from ancient Chinese texts devoted to the topic, is certainly impressive:
- It activates blood circulation.
- It stimulates thinking and alertness.

- It facilitates the elimination of alcohol and other harmful substances (fats and nicotine, for example).
- It boosts the body's resistance to disease.
- It improves metabolism and facilitates the supply of oxygen to vital organs.
- It inhibits dental decay.
- It purifies and strengthens the skin, helping to preserve a youthful appearance.
- It prevents or alleviates anemia.
- It clarifies the urine and facilitates elimination.
- It strengthens and brightens the eyes.
- It combats the effects of summer heat.
- It aids digestion.
- It eases limb and joint pain.
- It diminishes mucus secretion.
- It alleviates fatigue and depression, and enhances a sense of well being.
- Finally, for all the reasons listed above, it prolongs life.

…today, these benefits are recognized in modern medicine

Modern scientific analysis supports these widely held perceptions of the benefits of tea. Today we know that caffeine gently stimulates the nervous and circulatory systems. The flavonoids (compounds rich in vitamins that reduce blood pressure) contained in green tea are four times more potent than vitamins C and E. They protect against free radicals and regulate the hormonal and cardiovascular systems. Consumption of just two or three cups of green tea a day can reduce cardiovascular risk by 40 percent.

Green tea is known to combat bad cholesterol and inhibits the absorption of fats during digestion. It helps the body to burn calories and facilitates weight loss.

Green tea is particularly rich in vitamin C, as well as A, B, E and K. Its leaves also provide potassium, magnesium, phosphorus, sodium, copper, chlorophyll, and fluoride, which protects against tooth decay and fights proliferation of bacteria. It also contains 20 percent fiber. Each of these components contributes to good health.

Once infused, cotton muslin tea sachets can be used as compresses to smooth fatigue lines or reduce puffiness under the eyes.

132

Recent studies show that green tea's antibacterial action is very effective for the entire body. Applied with compresses, green tea can also be used to care for minor injuries.

Studies carried out by Drs. Fujiki and Saitama in Japan at the Cancer Research Institute have demonstrated the benefits of green tea consumption in the prevention of cancer. Isolating epigallocatechin gallate (EGCG), a substance which seems to be among the most effective yet discovered in combating cancer, the researchers noted that it inhibited the development of lung metastases and of carcinogenic cells in the stomach, intestine, liver, and skin. They also found it diminished the toxic effects of tobacco smoke. Dr. Fujiki suggests drinking six or seven cups of green tea a day, preferably in the morning and at midday, allowing a level teaspoon per cup. This regime is also helpful for those wishing to reduce or eliminate their coffee consumption.

An infusion of Samurai green tea and rose petals applied to the skin stimulates a sense of well being and freshness.

The benefits of green tea do not stop there. A Chinese study recently showed that green tea improved the density of bone mass. This effect is most noticeable among subjects who have been drinking green tea for ten or more years. The spinal column, the neck of the femur, and generally the entire skeletal system are strengthened.

A beverage rich in antioxidants, with no contraindications

The Organization for Nutritional Education (O.N.E.) has recently added tea to its list of foods rich in antioxidants, stating that "tea leaves contain a high level of natural components with antioxidant properties, very much like fruits and vegetables." This observation is confirmed by a study performed at Tufts University in Boston, which compared the antioxidant powers of tea leaves with those of 22 other plant foods including broccoli, garlic, onions, corn, and carrots. Tea leaves were ranked first!

Everyone can enjoy and experience the benefits provided by green tea. It may be sipped throughout the day, beginning with breakfast, with no known contraindications. Because of its high vitamin C content, some vitamin deficient individuals may experience a reaction if they drink tea after 5:00 PM. This problem disappears after supplements of this vitamin are absorbed. Those highly sensitive to caffeine should avoid tea consumption late in the day.

Green tea's role as a beauty aid

Green tea is used today in preparing many beauty and skin care products, such as these Elizabeth Arden bath salts (left), as well as room fragrances, such as these green tea incense sticks and spirals (below).

Tea's most invaluable role as a beauty aid is its contribution to overall good health. Its vitamins and antioxidant properties help to slow the aging process. Numerous prominent cosmetic laboratories use tea as an ingredient in their creams, proving that the plant is equally beneficial to the skin. Some products combine skin care, aromatherapy, and fragrance. Others use the soothing, relaxing qualities of green tea in their body care and bath lines.

The tradition of green tea in cosmetics

All of these laboratories share the desire to use this plant, whose origins go back to the beginning of recorded history, in alliance with modern science. Each of the studies sponsored by the major cosmetic companies conclude that green tea provides numerous benefits for the skin. Elizabeth Arden's marketing director recently explained that their "Green Tea" body care and bath line is at the forefront of skin care, aromatherapy, and fragrance.

The prestigious house of Bulgari believes that green tea fosters harmony in daily life and well-being. It offers the extraordinary green tea "Eau Parfumée," which has been created out a profound understanding of the culture of tea and a reverence for its rituals. A precious extract of green tea, known as a relaxant, is also used in the company's body care product line. The tea sachets for the bath are recommended for the soothing properties of vegetable extracts they contain.

Origins has released a white tea product called "A Perfect World—Skin Protector with White Tea."

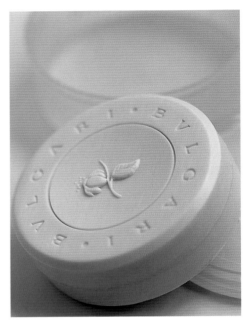

The company's mission is to rediscover ancient recipes based on plants and use them in contemporary products.

Other brands, including Guerlain, Roger & Gallet, and l'Artisan Parfumeur, have created their own green tea lines. These products are of the highest quality, and very refreshing and simple to use.

"Homemade" beauty recipes

You can concoct recipes at home that offer the benefits of green tea. A tan will last longer if you pat your face with a green tea infusion that has been infused for a long time.

If your eyes have dark circles or feel tired, apply a compress of green tea leaves to your eyelids in the morning to reduce swelling.

After removing makeup in the evening, use tea as a toner: just infuse Japanese Sencha green tea for about three minutes in 160°F water. The infusion will keep in a sealed bottle in the refrigerator. Prepare a fresh infusion every two or three days.

You may also save green tea leaves that have been infused and apply them to your face for ten minutes before rinsing. Green tea helps the skin resist external pollutants, because it is rich in antioxidants and protects against the formation of free radicals.

Above: Bulgari green tea perfume (left); Silver Tip White Tea from Origins, a cosmetics company that promotes beauty from within (center); Bulgari green tea soap (right).

Right: Green tea exfoliant for the body from Elizabeth Arden.

138

Enjoying tea
all day long

Green tea is well known as a helpful tool for weight loss. It is an excellent diuretic and an effective remedy for water retention and cholesterol buildup. A good appetite suppressant, green tea helps the body burn fat. Drinking tea throughout the day can therefore help fight weight gain. Remember that green tea is very rich in vitamins, particularly vitamin C. You should select your tea carefully according to the time of day you are drinking it.

In the morning, prepare a generous amount of green tea (Japanese Sencha O.P. or Chinese Lung Ching) or black tea (Yunnan Tuo Cha or Pu-erh), and enjoy it throughout the morning. Yunnan Tuo Cha and Pu-erh, both known for their "moist earth" flavor, come from the Yunnan province and are known for their fat-burning properties.

With lunch or in the early afternoon, select teas lower in caffeine, such as Bancha Hojicha, a flavorful roasted tea that is an ideal accompaniment to a meal of fish.

In the late afternoon, choose semi-fermented teas that are even lower in caffeine so that your sleep patterns will not be disturbed. Blue-green China or Formosa oolongs are particularly mild.

How to decaffeinate tea

For 1 quart of tea

5 teaspoons of your choice of tea

1 quart of water

Christine Dattner

Heat the water in a pot.

Place the tea leaves in a paper filter or cloth tea sock.

Pour the water over the tea and immediately pour off the first infusion. This process removes 80 percent of the caffeine.

Repeat the operation, allowing the leaves to steep for several minutes according to taste.

140

Green tea with mint
to aid digestion

For 1 quart of tea

1 quart mineral water
with a neutral pH

3 or 4 teaspoons China Gunpowder
green tea

10 mint leaves

3 sugar cubes

Christine Dattner

Green tea stimulates the intestines, and mint improves digestion

Put the tea, the mint and the sugar together in a teapot. Heat water to 175°F and pour into the teapot. Allow to infuse about five minutes before drinking. ▸

Green tea compresses
for the eyes

For 10 compresses

1 cup mineral water

1 teaspoon green tea

Christine Dattner

Green tea compresses are effective treatments for circles, puffiness, and fatigue lines.

Heat the water to 160°F and pour it into a teapot. Add the green tea and infuse three to five minutes. Strain. Allow to cool, then refrigerate the infusion for one hour.

Pour three or four drops on each compress and apply the compresses, well chilled, to the eyelids for five to ten minutes.

Practical Information on Green Tea

From Japan's Matcha, Genmaicha, or Gyokuro to China's Taimu Long Zhu, Tian Hua or Lung Ching, from Taiwan's Black Dragon or Chung Pou Chong to India's Pearl of India or Darjeeling Oolong, to South America's Mate, these teas have flavors and energetic and therapeutic qualities characteristic of green tea . . . We offer here a taste guide to the greatest green teas and their cousins—white teas and blue-green teas—from all over the world. Savor these twenty-five superb leafs and their subtle, delicate aromas.

Matcha

A powdered green tea from Japan.
In the Japanese tea ceremony, *Cha No Yu*, Matcha is whisked with water. It has recently been included as an ingredient in various recipes.
Its liquor is pale green, dense, powerful, and concentrated. On the palate, it has a vegetal finish with a slight aftertaste of spinach.
Matcha is particularly rich in vitamin C.
Water temperature: 160°F.

Genmaicha

A Sencha green tea from Japan. This variety is a blend of tea, toasted rice kernels, and popped corn.
Its liquor is pale green with a somewhat smoky flavor. A delicious accompaniment to a meal of fish at lunchtime.
Water temperature: 160°F.
Infusion time: three to four minutes.

Gyokuro (Jukoro)

A green tea from Japan.
Gyokuro ("Precious Dew") is indisputably the most exquisite of Japanese teas. Its leaves are exceptionally fine and very dark in color. Its liquor is emerald green with a delicate, flowery flavor. Gyokuro is very rich in vitamins.
An ideal drink during the morning, with lunch, and in the early afternoon.
Water temperature: 140°F.
Infusion time: 45 seconds to one minute.

Bancha Hojicha

A roasted green tea from Japan. Its leaves are very large and its liquor is green, verging on pale yellow. It has a very fresh, lightly toasted flavor.
Ideal after lunch.
Water temperature: 160°F.
Infusion time: four to five minutes.

Sencha O.P.

A green tea from Japan.
Its leaves are green and flat. The liquor is pale with a light taste. Sencha O.P. is rich in vitamins.
Ideal for drinking in the morning, with lunch, and in the early afternoon.
Water temperature: 160°F.
Infusion time: three minutes.

Sencha Yamato

A green tea from Japan.
Yamato is the finest Sencha variety, an exceptionally high quality tea. Its liquor is green and its flavor is very mild.
Ideal for drinking in the morning, with lunch, and in the early afternoon.
Water temperature: 160°F.
Infusion time: three minutes.

Taïmu Long Zhu

A white tea from China.
Taïmu Long Zhu ("Jade Bead") is a lovely tea with a mellow flavor and a very pale liquor.
May be enjoyed throughout the day.
Water temperature: 160°F.
Can withstand three or four infusions.

Jade Needle

A white tea from China.
A delightful variety with a very pale liquor and a delicate flavor.
May be enjoyed throughout the day.
Water temperature: 160°F.
Can withstand three or four infusions.

Jade Tower

A white tea from China.
Each "tower" is formed from approximately
100 buds. The liquor is very pale and its
flavor fresh.
May be enjoyed throughout the day.
Water temperature: 175°F.
Can withstand three or four infusions.

Yu Huan

A white tea from China.
Yu Huan ("Jade Ring") is a lovely tea with a
pale liquor and a very fresh "meadow" flavor.
May be enjoyed throughout the day.
Water temperature: 175°F.
You may infuse the loose leaves three or four
times in the cup.

Yin Zhen

A white tea from China.
Yin Zhen (Silver Needle) is a magnificent
variety rich in vitamins. Its liquor is very pale,
and its flavor is flowery and sweet.
May be enjoyed throughout the day.
Water temperature: 160°F.
Infusion time: three to four minutes.

Huang Shan Mu Dang

A sculpted green tea from China.
This tea, formed by handknotting about
200 buds on a thread, resembles a flower.
Its liquor is pale, with a mellow, subtle flavor.
May be enjoyed throughout the day.
Water temperature: 160°F.
Place the leaves in the bottom of a cup and
watch them unfurl and open like a flower.
Can withstand up to ten infusions.

Tian Hua

A sculpted white tea from China.
This tea, formed by handknotting about
200 buds on a thread, resembles a flower.
Its liquor is pale with a delicate flavor.
Water temperature: 160°F.
Place the leaves in the bottom of a cup and
watch them unfurl and open like a flower.
May be infused up to ten times.

Ti Kuan Yin

A blue-green tea from China.
Also known as Iron Goddess of Mercy, this
tea is an oolong with an amber liquor and
a mellow, flowery flavor.
An ideal tea at the end of the day.
Water temperature: 175°F.
Infusion time: five to seven minutes.

Gunpowder

A green tea from China.
Gunpowder has a pale green liquor and a very strong flavor.
It is used primarily for mint tea infusions.
Water temperature: 175°F.
Infuse the leaves loose in a teapot.

Lung Ching

A green tea from China.
Also known as Dragon Well, this is a very revitalizing tea rich in vitamins. Its leaves are large and attractive. Its liquor is pale with a very fresh flavor.
Ideal for drinking in the morning, with lunch, and in the early afternoon.
Water temperature: 160°F.
Infusion time: two to three minutes.

Yunnan Silver Hill

A green tea from China.
This delightful variety is the finest of the Yunnans. Its has a pale liquor with a flowery taste.
Ideal for drinking in the morning, with lunch, and in the early afternoon.
Water temperature: 175°F.
Infusion time: three minutes.

Pai Mu Tan

A white tea from China.
Also known as White Peony, this excellent tea is rich in vitamins. A cup of Pai Mu Tan provides the vitamin equivalent of ten oranges. Its liquor is very pale and the flavor is flowery.
Ideal for drinking in the morning, with lunch, and in the early afternoon.
Water temperature: 175°F.
Infusion time: seven to 20 minutes.
The leaves may be infused again for a late afternoon beverage.

Black Dragon

A blue-green tea from Formosa.
This oolong is Formosa's finest variety. Its liquor is orange and its mellow flavor has a chestnut finish.
Ideal at the end of the day.
Water temperature: 175°F.
Infusion time: five to seven minutes

Chung Pou Chong

A blue-green tea from Formosa.
Also known as Bao Zhong, this oolong has long dark leaves. Its liquor is orange with a mellow, delicate flavor.
Ideal at the end of the day.
Water temperature: 175°F.
Infusion time: five to seven minutes.

Dung Ding

A blue-green tea from Formosa.
Also known as Frozen Summit, this is a very
fine variety that comes from the mountain
of the same name. Its liquor is orange with
a delicate taste.
Ideal at the end of the day.
Water temperature: 175°F.
Infusion time: five minutes.

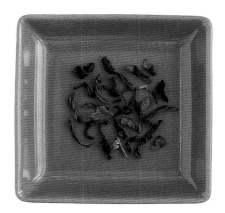

Formosa Oolong

A blue-green tea from Formosa.
Its liquor is orange, and its flavor is mellow
with a chestnut finish.
Ideal at the end of the day.
Water temperature: 175°F.
Infusion time: five to seven minutes.

Pearl of India

A white tea from India.
This lovely variety comes from the
Gopaldhara plantation in the Darjeeling region.
Its liquor is pale yellow, and its flavor is very
mellow and fresh.
Ideal for drinking from late morning to
midday.
Water temperature: 175°F.
You may infuse this tea three or four times
loose in the cup.

Darjeeling Oolong

A blue-green tea from India.
This excellent variety comes from the
Gopaldhara plantation in the Darjeeling region.
Its liquor is pale yellow, and its flavor has
a finish of unripened fruit.
May be enjoyed throughout the day.
Water temperature: 175°F.
Infusion time: three minutes.

Maté

Maté is an energizing beverage popular in
South America. Its flavor and properties are
very close to those of green tea. Its liquor
is green with a slightly bitter flavor.
Ideal for drinking in the morning, with lunch,
and in the early afternoon.
Water temperature: 175°F.
Infuse the loose leaves. Traditionally, maté is
placed in a wooden vessel and barely simmering
water is poured over. The beverage is sipped
through a little straw, which has its own filter.

Teapots and their various styles

急須

Crimson glazed Chinese clay teapot

Chinese clay teapot with built-in filter

Enameled Chinese clay teapot

Yixing clay Chinese teapot with built-in filter

Dragon-shaped Yixing clay Chinese teapot

Non-drip Denby enameled stoneware
English teapot

Enamel English teapot, reproduced by Arthur Wood, 1930 mold

Porcelain Russian teapot from a manufacturer
in Saint Petersburg

Clay Japanese teapot with metal filter

Cast-iron Fuji Yama Japanese teapot
with metal filter

Cast-iron Japanese teapot
with metal filter

Silver-plate Moroccan teapot

Glass German teapot
with built-in glass filter

Les Contes
de Thé

Today, Contes de Thé exports all over the world.

Tea drinkers are very demanding connoisseurs and so the quality of our selection and our creations must always be the best. I have worked for the last twenty-five years toward this end, driven by a love and passion for tea.

Below a list of addresses for tea salons, cafés, restaurants, hotels, and tea shops.

TEA SALONS AND SHOPS

These salons de thé serve loose leaf tea and offer a varied choice of "classic" and "flavored" teas. Tea is presented in cast iron or porcelain teapots with cotton or paper filters that are ideal for infusing.

BAMBOO TEA HOUSE
221 Yale Avenue
Claremont, CA 91711-4725
(909) 626-7668
This connoisseur tea house sells some of the best loose-leaf teas. Every day a different tea is brewed for you to sample and you can learn the Chinese, Japanese, British, and Yerba Mate tea history and ceremony from their knowledgeable staff.

CHADO TEA HOUSE
8422 1/2 West Third Street
Los Angeles, CA 90048-4112
(323) 655-2056
One of the best tea rooms in Los Angeles. Boasts a wide variety of black, green, and flavored teas.

CHING CHING CHA
1063 Wisconsin Avenue NW
Washington DC 20007
(202) 333-8288
The restaurant's focus is on tea: the pot of water boiling in the center of the table, the careful selection from the many pages of teas, the instructions in brewing--different for each variety--and finally the sipping from a tiny covered porcelain.

THE FOUR SEASONS HOTEL
57 East 57th Street
New York, NY 10021
(212) 758-5700
If you're looking for something more traditional, chef Susan Weaver offers a tempting assortment of sandwiches, freshly baked scones with Devonshire cream, and dainty pastries.

GREEN TEA
19 Blanchard Road
Cambridge, MA 02138-1010
(617) 864-8326

GREEN TEA CAFE
45 Mott Street
New York, NY 10013
(212) 693-2888
This Chinese Tea House provides Frothy Green Tea and Pearl Tapioca.

ENG'S TEA HOUSE
710 North Old Rand Road
Lake Zurich, IL 60047-2210
(847) 438-6401

HAWAIIAN TEA CO
400 Hookahi Street
Wailuku, HI 96793-1467
(808) 573-0233

HEARTBEAT
149 East 49th Street
New York, NY 10021
(212) 407-2900
With the advent of "tea sommelier" James Labe, the tea ritual at New York's W Hotel has reached new heights. He and chef Michel Nischan have collaborated on two four-course afternoon tea-tasting menus—one for black, the other for green and oolong. Labe offers eleven loose-leaf teas, each steeped in a small porcelain pot according to the character of the tea, then decanted into a fresh pot, avoiding that stewed brew.

IN PURSUIT OF TEA INC.
224 Roebling Street
Brooklyn, NY 11211
(718) 302-0780
Sebastian Beckwith specializes in "cuisine level teas" for New York diners who like to match specific teas with specific meals.

JAPANESE TEA GARDEN
Golden Gate Park
San Francisco, CA 94111-3404
(415) 752 1171
Enjoy the flowers and take time out for tea at this Japanese-themed attraction in Golden Gate Park.

KAI RESTAURANT AND ITO EN TEA STORE
822 Madison Avenue
New York, NY 10021
(212) 988-7111
In Japanese, the word KAI signifies meeting or gathering. Kaiseki cuisine has its origins in the temples of Kyoto over 500 years ago as delicate foods to accompany a tea ceremony. At KAI, the ancient way of kaiseki is re-energized with a modern spirit that celebrates the elemental purity of traditional Japanese cuisine.

MAUI SUN TEA
210 Kawehi Place
Kula, HI 96790-7804
(808) 876-1188

SAINT'S ALP TEAHOUSE
51 Mott Street
New York, NY 10013
(212) 766-9889
Order any of the cold frothy milk teas with tapioca pearls and get a sip-by-sip thrill from sucking the gummy black balls up through the colorful, oversized straw. Other liquid delicacies include fruit, nectar, and classical tea based beverages.

SAFFRON
279A Newbury Street
Boston, MA 02116
(617) 536-9766
Saffron's signature desserts accompany traditional teas from the Far East.

T SALON
11 East 20th Street
New York, NY 10003
(212) 925-3700
This three-story salon in Chelsea sells more than 100 blended teas, plus teapots, tea-flavored condiments, and herbal elixirs. Enthusiasts can sign up for tea-making and Japanese tea ceremony classes.

TAMARIND
41-43 East 22nd Street
New York, NY 10010
(212) 674-7400
The Tamarind Tea Room offers a range of teas from Asia with recommended Indian influenced snacks and pastries.

TEA BOX
693 Fifth Avenue
New York, NY 10022
(212) 350-0180
The Tea Box Cafe at Takashimaya offers more than 36 teas kinds of tea from Japan, China, and England.

TEAISM TEA SHOP
400 Eighth St. NW
Washington, DC 20009
(202) 638-7740
Located next to the tea room, the shop features a large selection of teapots imported from China and Japan. A sea of loose-leaf teas as well as tea cups, boxes, and trays.

TEANY
90 Rivington Street
New York, NY 10002
(212) 475-9190
This tea-green canteen serves almost 100 blends of tea. Moby's fans will recognize his Little Idiot alter ego in the mosaic-tiled floor, a humanistic counterpart to the pair of teapot-headed robots with teaspoon hands.

TEN REN TEA & GINSENG COMPANY
2247 South Wentworth Ave
Chicago, IL 60616-2011
(312) 842-1171
The most complete selection of Chinese tea around. Ten Ren holds free tea drinking classes to help you distinguish different kinds of tea, stop by one of the stores and they will welcome you with a cup of hot green tea.

OUR PLACE SHANGHAI TEA GARDEN
141 East 55th Street
New York, NY 10022
(212) 753-3900

THE PIERRE HOTEL
2 East 61st Street
New York, NY 10021
(212) 838-8000
A New York classic, the Pierre continues to serve a traditional tea every afternoon.

WILD LILY TEA MARKET
545 East 12th Street
New York, NY 10009
212-598-9097
An oasis of oolongs and Darjeelings, the tea room offers a selection of senchas, lapsang souchongs, and caffeine-free herbal tisanes. Besides selling leaves by the ounce, they offer a line of stylish products made both for and from tea: green-tea soap, business cards, and odor-fighting insoles for your shoes.

YOSHIDA-YA
2909 Webster Street
San Francisco, CA 94123
(415) 346-3431
From the pot of green tea that magically appears on your table to the gently paced service, Yoshida-Ya offers a quiet retreat.

B.O.P. : Broken Orange Pekoe; a broken leaf tea

Cha No Yu : Japanese tea ceremony

First flush : first harvest of the year

F.O.P. : Flowery Orange Pekoe; a tea made from top leaves

F.T.G.F.O.P. : Finest Tips Golden Flowery Orange Pekoe; a tea with many fine buds

Golden Flowery Orang Pekoe (G.F.O.P.) : a high quality tea with golden whole leaves

Gong Fu Cha : Chinese tea ceremony

In-between : intermediate harvest between the first and the second

O.P. : Orange Pekoe; tea with whole leaves

Pekoe : white-haired or downy

Second flush : second harvest or plucking

(S.F.G.F.O.P.) Special Finest Golden Flowery Orange Pekoe; Special Finest Golden Flowery Orange Pekoe ; an exceptional variety !

(T.G.F.O.P.) Tips Golden Flowery Orange Pekoe; Tips Golden Flowery Orange Pekoe ; a high quality tea with buds and golden whole leaves

TIPS : white shoots, bud leaves from the tea plant

Acknowledgments

- Elizabeth Arden
- Nicolas Boussin, Christelle Vandaele,
  la Grande Épicerie
- Thierry Bridron, Philippe Renard,
  hôtel Lutétia
- Bulgari
- Henri Burgos, les Délices du roy
- Michèle Carles
- Philippe and Sylvie Charpentier,
  les Jardins d'Hélény
- C.M.O.
- Béatrice Cointreau, Champagne Gosset
- Comptoir français de l'Orient et de la Chine
- Paul Conan, Stéphane Henriot,
  Jérôme Nagat, Aux mille délices
- The Conran Shop
- Walter Deshayes, Hélène Huret,
  Bernardaud
- Esteban
- Fauchon
- Sandrine Ganem
- Michel Hache, hôtel Ambassador
- Fatema Hal, le Mansouria
- Marlène Heurtematte, Les Contes de thé
- Étienne Jorge, Oolong Shan
- Kazé, dans le vent
- Emmanuel Laporte, les Feuilles libres
- Michel Lentz, hôtel Royal Parc Évian
- Robert Linxe, La Maison du chocolat
- Soraya et Renato Lolli, Marhaba
- Louiselio
- Patrick Loustalot-Barbe, l'Artisan de saveurs
- Massimo Mori, Emporio Armani
- L'Occitane
- Origins
- La Paresse en douce
- Olivier Scala
- Le Web Store

All of the photographs are by Sophie
Boussahba except

Réunion des musées nationaux :
pages 10–11, 18–19.
Giraudon/The Bridgeman Art Librairy :
pages 15, 20, 28.
Lipton : page 16.
Roger-Viollet : page 19.
Hoa-Qui/Explorer : pages 21 (P. de Wilde),
24–25 (J. Horner), 26 (Globe Press), 29, 30
(P. Thomas), 32a (J. Horner), 32b (D. Huot),
34–35 (J.-L. Dugast), 37 (C. Vaisse), 38a
(J.-L. Dugast), 39b (P. Bernard), 40a (P. Wang),
40b (Glob Press), 46 (J. Jaffre), 54 (G. Bouttin),
56–57 (C. Vaisse), 58 (E. Sampers), 59
(D. Huot), 82 (M. Renaudeau).
Diaf : pages 33 (J.-D. Sudres), 38b, 39a
(A. Even), 44 (J.-D. Sudres), 60–61 (Eurasia
Press).
Christine Dattner : page 36, 80, 81.
Getty Images France : pages 50–51 (Mahaux).